DEATH BY DECISION

THE MEDICAL, MORAL, AND LEGAL DILEMMAS OF EUTHANASIA

By
Jerry B. Wilson

THE WESTMINSTER PRESS
Philadelphia

Book design by Dorothy Alden Smith

Published by The Westminster Press®
Philadelphia, Pennsylvania

PRINTED IN THE UNITED STATES OF AMERICA

Library of Congress Cataloging in Publication Data

Wilson, Jerry B., 1939–
  Death by decision.

  Based on the author's thesis, Emory University.
  Includes bibliographical references.
  1. Euthanasia. 2. Terminal care. I. Title.
R726.W55   174'.24   74-34482
ISBN 0-664-20729-4

TO OUR PARENTS

Stella H. Wilson

Paul B. Wilson (1910–1970)

Ruby R. and W. Clyde Templeton

CONTENTS

FOREWORD

by E. Clinton Gardner

The question of euthanasia has received increased attention in recent years as the result of the dramatic advances that have been made in medical technology. While the problem itself is an ancient one, rooted in the conflict between the duty to relieve suffering and the duty to preserve human life, it has assumed new proportions with the advent of modern medicine. Decisions to determine the time and the circumstances of one's dying have become both more frequent and more complex in view of the capacity of modern medical science to sustain biological life almost indefinitely by artificial means.

This new technological capacity poses serious moral issues concerning the quality of life that can be maintained through the employment of such technology. It also raises far-reaching questions regarding the costs of terminal medical care, the rights of the patient, the need for an updated definition of death, and the allocation of scarce medical resources. These and related issues have important implications in the field of law as well as medicine. They pertain both to the rights of the individual and to the welfare of society.

In its original form the present study was presented by Jerry Wilson as a doctoral dissertation at Emory University

under the title "The Moral, Medical, and Legal Dimensions
of Euthanasia." From its inception, the project was based
on two primary assumptions. First, it was recognized that
euthanasia in the broad sense of that term raises problems
which cut across a number of interrelated fields. Hence,
any adequate approach to such problems needs to include
insights from each of these perspectives. Decisions related
to the election of death are not simply medical decisions in
the technical sense; they are also choices which are deeply
influenced by religious, moral, legal, and economic considerations. Medical decisions are made within the framework of
legislation that defines the responsibility of the physician to
the patient in terms of law and establishes public policy
with regard both to the quality and the general availability
of health care services. Decisions related to the use of
"extraordinary" procedures for maintaining life are severely
limited by the economic resources available to the patient
and the patient's family as well as by the resources that are
at the disposal of the physician through various agencies. In
addition to the medical, legal, and economic factors,
euthanasia also involves fundamental ethical issues related
to the nature and limits of the physician's responsibility to
his patient, the rights of the patient, and the responsibility
of the patient's family as well as that of society in the care of
the dying.

The second assumption underlying the original study was
the belief that the questions of euthanasia and the care of
the terminally ill are at bottom moral problems. The moral
dimensions of euthanasia do not exist alongside the medical,
the legal, and the economic dimensions; rather, the former
so permeate and condition the latter that even these cannot
be adequately perceived unless they are understood also in
a normative ethical context. Hence, a major purpose of the
present study is to bring the various perspectives—medical,
legal, and moral—together in search of a more responsible

health policy for the treatment of the terminally ill. To this end, Wilson proposes certain moral guidelines for terminal medical practice and also related legal norms for legislation affecting such practice in a pluralistic society.

An increasingly large portion of present-day society is not only affected by, but also involved as participants in, decisions related to the care of the terminally ill over long periods of time. This book promises to be a valuable resource for lay persons seeking a fuller understanding of the problems involved in such relationships. It should also provide assistance to specialists in the fields of medicine, law, and theology who are seeking new approaches to these problems, approaches that are at once more comprehensive and more human.

In view of the interdisciplinary nature of this study, Wilson seeks to establish a common ground for the consideration of the moral aspects of euthanasia. Following a suggestion of Henry David Aiken, Wilson distinguishes between several levels at which the morality of euthanasia may be discussed: viz., the expressive-evocative, the moral, the ethical, and the post-ethical levels. With the aid of this analytical device, the author is able to distinguish between discussions of the morality of euthanasia which take place primarily on the basis of unreflective feeling, discussions which take place on the level of conventional morality as expressed in existing legislation and prevailing medical practice, and those which proceed on a more normative, critical level at which the prevailing policies and practices are themselves evaluated. This third "level of moral discourse" points ultimately beyond itself to certain "post-ethical" commitments (the realm of faith) in which moral and ethical judgments about values and duties are finally grounded. The search for more clearly defined and more adequate criteria for "death by decision" must proceed on the ethical and post-ethical levels, not simply on the emotional and conventional (moral) levels. Nevertheless, such a differentiation of various planes at which discussion of euthanasia does in actuality take place enables the reader to enter into the analytical process on one level (feeling, law, conventional medical practice, or faith commitment) and relate his perception from that standpoint to other dimensions of the problem which are disclosed at other levels of experience. It should be noted in this connection that while Wilson's own approach to euthanasia is from the standpoint of Christian ethics, the ethical perspective that he develops takes the pluralism of our contemporary society seriously into account.

PREFACE

Science so extends and enriches our lives that we are inclined to accept its progress without reservations. Nevertheless, the benefits of our science and technology are not always unmixed blessings. They often create complex dilemmas which can only be resolved by hard decisions. The most difficult of these problems are not simply theoretical or technical questions requiring additional research. They are, instead, the moral questions connected with research and with the application of new information and skills. In many cases, these problems expose the inadequacies of our conventional moral and legal systems. When this occurs, it is necessary to update our standards and institutions in order to come to terms with the moral crises posed by scientific and technological developments.

Moral questions that arise as a result of advances in medical science and technology are especially serious. Perhaps the most complex problems are posed by the physician's ability to exercise extensive control over the processes of life and death. From a strictly medical standpoint, life and death decisions have become routine. From a moral point of view, however, such choices are seldom easy. The dilemma is particularly acute when traditional medical ethics impose conflicting requirements.

The question of euthanasia is one of a broad spectrum of moral problems of terminal medical care. It arises in those cases in which the duty to relieve suffering conflicts with the obligation to preserve life. In some respects, this question is closely related to that of abortion. In fact, when a pregnancy is terminated because the fetus is defective, abortion may constitute what can be referred to as fetal euthanasia. The question of abortion for eugenic reasons, or as a form of birth control, or out of consideration for the mother, however, is an altogether different matter. The crucial difference is that it is concerned with factors other than regard for the primary life that is taken. The question of terminating "hopeless" life in order to secure vital organs for lives that can be "saved" differs from the question of euthanasia in the same way.

This study deals with the problem of the morality of euthanasia from a theocentric perspective. It examines both the medical and the legal dimensions of this question. In so doing, it takes into account not only the requirements of law and of professional medical ethics but also the ways in which decisions are made in the context of concrete cases. These standards and practices are analyzed in order to discover the underlying ethical principles. These in turn are evaluated and interpreted in relation to theocentric love. This serves as the basis for Christian medical ethics to transform moral norms for terminal medical care.

The primary purpose of this study is to offer moral guidelines for medical decisions and for legal norms for medical practice in cases involving hopeless suffering. Until recently, this question has received relatively little attention in theological ethics. It is hoped this study will make a constructive contribution to the growing debate. Its conclusions are not intended as final "solutions" for the problem of euthanasia. Instead, they are recommendations which are based on an understanding of the requirements of love in response to the needs and claims of patients who are suffering and dying.

Because of the nature of the subject, there will be disagreements with my proposals. This I welcome. The scope of the problem makes it impossible to take into account every facet. I have attempted to come to terms with the more crucial issues involved. For the limitations of my work, I am responsible. For its merits, I am indebted to those who assisted me in preparing the book. I am especially grateful to my wife for her patience and support while I worked on the manuscript first as a dissertation and then for its publication. I also appreciate the advice and encouragement of Dr. E. Clinton Gardner, chairman of the Department of Religion and Society of Emory University, who served as the adviser for my dissertation. In addition, a note of thanks is due to the following members of the faculty of Emory University who served on my dissertation committee: Dr. Theodore R. Weber, Associate Professor of Social Ethics, Dr. Quentin L. Hand, Associate Professor of Psychology and Pastoral Counseling, Dr. Arthur P. Richardson, Dean of Emory University School of Medicine, Dr. G. Stanley Joslin, Charles Howard Candler Professor of Law, and Dr. James T. Laney, Dean of the Candler School of Theology. Finally, I wish to express my appreciation to Jacksonville State University, the administration, faculty, and students, with whom I share in the commerce of ideas.

JERRY B. WILSON

Jacksonville, Alabama

1
EUTHANASIA:
PAST AND PRESENT

The question of euthanasia is one of the most difficult moral problems that arise in the context of terminal medical care. Because suffering and death are perennial, this is an ancient problem. Nevertheless, it now occurs with greater frequency and is much more difficult to resolve because of advances in the art and science of medicine. This chapter examines the ways in which this question has been understood and dealt with in the past. It provides insight into the conflicting opinions in our society with regard to the morality of euthanasia.

The mental image created by the term "euthanasia" is often that of a doctor or a relative helping, perhaps clandestinely, a hopelessly moribund patient to cut short his agony in death or deliberately terminating the life of a malformed infant, thus "mercifully" delivering it from lifelong suffering. In this image, attention is focused not so much on death, which may be considered merciful, as on the act and motive by which death is brought about. Originally, however, "euthanasia" referred to the "easy death" rather than to the means, act, or practice by which it was effected.

In classical Greek literature, the adjective *euthanatos*, from the adverb *eu* ("well") and the noun *thanatos* ("death"), connoted an easy and happy death, an ideal and coveted end to a full and pleasant life. The same meaning was preserved in Roman literature. This is reflected in Suetonius' account of the death of Caesar Augustus: "He expired suddenly, . . . dying a very easy death, and such as he himself had always wished for." [1] Under the influence of the Stoics, "euthanasia" was also used to describe a "noble" death, the fitting climax to a valiant life. Here again, death occurred in keeping with the honorable style of life, and there was no question of the means by which death occurred.

By the seventeenth century, however, the same term that was applied to the act of dying peacefully was also applied to the medical art by which this was accomplished. While there was as yet no connection between euthanasia and killing a patient in order to relieve his suffering, treatment to permit patients to die easily was preferred over efforts to prolong the lives of the suffering and dying. Francis Bacon, for example, admonished doctors "to acquire the skill and to bestow the attention whereby the dying may pass more easily and quickly out of life." [2]

In the eighteenth and nineteenth centuries, "euthanasia" continued to refer to easy death and to medical care for the dying. The former meaning is expressed, for example, in Byron's *Euthanasia*, which was published in 1812. The latter meaning is reflected in the medical literature of the period. By the end of the nineteenth century, with the first movements to legalize mercy killing, "euthanasia" was being used to refer to the taking of life in order to end suffering. This does not mean that this practice is of such a recent origin. It suggests, however, that in order to understand the question of euthanasia (mercy killing) from a historical perspective, it is necessary to study the history of euthanasia (easy death) as a rationale for allowing the suffering to die and as a justification for taking their lives.

THE ANCIENT WORLD

There are numerous indications that in Greek culture the practice of euthanasia, in the sense of mercy killing, was not an exceptional occurrence. Instead, it seems to have been an accepted and prevalent affair. To comprehend fully the extent to which mercy killing took place and the ways in which it was justified, one must view its practice in relation to the then-current religious and secular medical practices. It is also important to see it in the context of the Greek conceptions of the value and purpose of human life. From this perspective, the conditions that were thought to warrant the termination of life can be understood.

Professional physicians of the classical period, such as the doctors depicted in the *Odyssey*, were itinerant. Like carpenters or minstrels, they had the status of craftsmen.[3] As in other trades, competition demanded that the medical artisan be successful. Success required that he be able to diagnose accurately and to cure quickly. Furthermore, it was considered his duty to treat only patients he could help. An example of this attitude is found in an essay in the *Hippocratic Collection* entitled "The Arts." Here the physician was required "to do away with the sufferings of the sick, to lessen the violence of their diseases, and to refuse to treat those who are overwhelmed by their diseases, realizing that in such cases medicine is powerless."[4] Because professional medical care was success-oriented and expensive, religious medicine in the sanctuaries of the various medical deities was the only recourse left for those who were considered beyond help or who could not afford professional services.[5]

The golden age of Greece was an age of reason and of changing values. With the expansion of medical knowledge and skill came an increasing recognition of the natural causes of illness and an unwillingness to ascribe disease to the wrath of the gods. With greater wealth and luxury, the Homeric values of glory and victory were replaced by the value of physical well-being. This was implicit in the Platonic principle of *kalokagathia*, the perfect balance of the physical and mental in man. In accordance with this ideal, health became the goal and standard of the good life, and illness became the curse that made beauty and happiness impossible. This emphasis accounts for the prestige of the Greek physicians in a society in which artisans were normally despised. It also explains some of the social, philosophical, and religious justifications for the practices of abandoning the deformed and terminating the lives of the incurably ill.

Such practices, however, were not always motivated solely by this ideal. Infanticide was enforced in Sparta as a crude form of eugenics designed primarily to create a healthy and vigorous people. Plutarch claimed that this practice was also motivated by concern for the individual. Although both Plato and Aristotle endorsed infanticide, neither suggested that a weak or deformed infant should be exposed out of mercy. There are several accounts of another ancient custom, if not a legal regulation, in Ceos which required those who reached the age of sixty to commit suicide. Aelian and Strabo described this as a utilitarian practice. Menander approved of it as a form of euthanasia.

According to Plato, Socrates insisted that the practice of medicine not only should have the interest of the state in view but should also operate for the good of the individual. In the *Republic*, Socrates praised Asclepius as a statesman who would neither lengthen out good-for-nothing lives nor have weak fathers begetting weaker sons. He criticized the wealthy and their doctors for wasting time and money trying to cure lingering and hopeless diseases. He especially condemned the physician Herodicus for having tortured himself and the rest of the world by "the invention of lingering death." [6]

In this culture, suicide, often by means of poison provided by physicians, was an everyday reality.[7] Athenian law did not sanction this practice as a release from pain or illness; nevertheless, it did not define suicide as a criminal offense. Such practices as burying the suicide in an isolated and unmarked grave or removing his hand were apparently done out of religious or superstitious fear of ghosts rather than as forms of punishment.[8] The best indication that suicides were committed as a kind of euthanasia is the fact that the practice was condemned by Pythagoreans, Platonists, Aristotelians, and Epicureans.

The Pythagoreans rigorously opposed suicide on the basis of their belief that man has been assigned to his post by the gods and is prohibited from deserting it regardless of the circumstances. Socrates referred to this belief as a "great mystery"; nevertheless, its influence on Socratic philosophy is evident. In the *Phaedo,* for example, Socrates argued that even "when a man is better off dead, he is not permitted to be his own benefactor." [9] The Hippocratic Oath, which became the basis for medical ethics in Western culture, reflects the Pythagorean orientation. According to Ludwig Edelstein, this oath was a "timely manifesto" which by its opposition attests to the prevalence of suicides that were aided and advised by physicians.[10]

Aristotle opposed suicide as contrary to the right rule of life and as an injustice to the state. Furthermore, he considered it cowardly for a man to take his own life in order to escape suffering. The Epicureans also exhorted the suffering not to give in easily to their illnesses and insisted on the folly of committing suicide out of fear of the terror of dying.[11] Although they believed that the soul ceased to exist at death, they did not value life at any cost. Epicurus urged men "to weigh carefully whether they would prefer death to come to them, or would themselves go to death." [12]

The Stoics, however, believed that life and death are "indifferent" for the wise man. Since the Stoic ideal was that life should be in accordance with nature, suicide became reasonable when this ideal was no longer possible because of pain, incurable disease, or physical abnormalities. On the basis of this view, Stoics were willing to relinquish life with only the slightest provocation. Zeno, the founder of this school, allegedly committed suicide simply because he sprained his finger. His successor, Cleanthes, gave up eating for two days at his doctor's request and chose to continue his journey toward death rather than turn back.[13] Because of the increasing popularity of Stoicism, this orientation greatly influenced later Aristotelianism and Epicureanism and undermined their opposition to suicide.[14]

The intellectual climate of the Roman Republic and the Roman Empire was less conducive to philosophical originality and creativity than was that of Greece. Pythagoreanism, Platonism, and Aristotelianism influenced Roman beliefs and values. Epicureanism and particularly Stoicism made an even greater impact. Attitudes toward suicide as a means to escape suffering reflect a synthesis of these divergent influences. This is evident in the writings of Epictetus, Cicero, Seneca, and Pliny the Elder. Seneca's position is especially representative of the general Stoic point of view:

> It makes a great deal of difference whether a man is lengthening his life or his death. But if the body is useless for service, why should one not free the struggling soul? Perhaps one ought to do this a little before the debt is due, lest, when it falls due, he may be unable to perform the act.[15]

Two movements were largely responsible for eroding this attitude. Neoplatonism, which arose in the third century

A.D., did not approve of suicide for any reason. Its opposition was based on the belief that man should not abandon the post assigned by God and on the belief that suicide adversely affected the life of the soul after death. Christianity also opposed the practice of suicide, which had long been accepted in Roman society. In this regard, it was influenced by Neoplatonism and by Judaism. Early Christians interpreted the commandment "Thou shalt not kill" to refer to suicide as well as to all other forms of taking human life. Although some of the church fathers made exceptions, allowing self-destruction in preference to apostasy or the loss of chastity, Augustine argued that no passage of Scripture could be found to sanction suicide in order to avoid temporal evils.

THE MIDDLE AGES AND THE MODERN ERA

Under the influence of Christianity, the value of life, which for the Greeks and Romans was determined by the quality of life, was reinterpreted to mean that life itself was valuable regardless of the circumstances. As a result of the dominance of the church, Stoicism was undermined. Suicide was denounced as diabolically inspired, and in ecclesiastical law, those who committed suicide were denied Christian burial. Although it had no immediate effect on the Theodosian and Justinian codes, the stigma placed by the church on suicide had a profound influence on civil legislation.

The popular fear of ghosts and the emotional revulsion against suicide also contributed to laws and customs inflicting retaliation on the corpses of suicides. Such practices in turn tended to reinforce the feelings that had produced them. Finally, the religious, social, and legal forces created a deterrent so powerful that, except under extreme conditions, the incidents of suicide were relatively rare during the Middle Ages.[16]

The medieval synthesis of the philosophical and theological arguments against suicide was created by Thomas Aquinas in the thirteenth century. According to Aquinas, suicide was sinful because it violated the commandment "Thou shalt not kill." He regarded it as the most dangerous of sins because it left no time for repentance. In support of his position, he summarized the Pythagorean, Platonic, Aristotelian, and Augustinian arguments against suicide. In the first place, he claimed that it was against the law of nature and contrary to charity which every man should have for himself. In the second place, he maintained that suicide was unlawful because each man belongs to the community. In the third place, he argued that taking one's own life was a sin against God because life is a gift of God and is subject to his power.[17]

The Reformation contributed to the breakdown of the vast authority held by the Roman Catholic Church during the Middle Ages. Nevertheless, it brought no change in the way in which suicide was regarded. The Reformers underscored the traditional theological arguments against its practice. At the same time, legal systems continued to oppose it.

During the period of the Reformation, the question of mercy killing was not discussed as a moral issue. In Martin Luther's *Table Talk*, however, there is an indication of the way in which the insane and the deformed were regarded and treated. According to three slightly variant accounts, Luther spoke of having recommended that a twelve-year-old congenitally abnormal boy be drowned. He explained that such a monster or idiot is only a lump of flesh, a *massa carnis*, that does not have a soul. He believed that the devil has the power so to corrupt people who have reason, body, and soul as to make them mute, deaf, and blind. According to Luther, the devil is in such changelings in the place of their souls.[18]

In Jewish literature, there is evidence that two curious forms of euthanasia were practiced in this period. According to Immanuel Jakobovits, it was believed that removing a pillow from beneath a dying person would enable the patient to die quickly. This practice was prohibited by a law that was recorded in the *Tur* by Jacob ben Asher in the fourteenth century. Nevertheless, the superstition and the practice continued into the seventeenth century and was not peculiar to the Jewish community. The second measure thought to bring about an easy death involved placing the synagogue keys under the pillow of the dying. This practice was condemned as a "magical remedy." [19]

Folktales and legends indicate that euthanasia may have been performed in Scotland, Wales, Ireland, and England. Such comments, made in jest by an aged invalid, as "I doot ye'll hae to tak the mason's mell (maul) to me," or about him, "Ay, he'll no dee till ye ca' out his horns (knock his brains out)," were common in Scotland well into the present century. These expressions may have been traces of a previously well established custom of killing the aged and the deformed by means of strangulation or a blow on the head. Similar practices of euthanasia in Brittany were reflected in expressions such as, "We will need to take the holy hammer to finish him," and in ceremonies in which this was ritually enacted as late as the nineteenth century. These suggest that death was once inflicted by means of a holy hammer, which was made of stone and usually kept in an old chapel in each district. When it was needed or requested, it was secured and "operated" by the oldest person in the village in order to crush the head of the dying while all of the inhabitants prayed. In all probability, however, the actual performance of euthanasia, both in Brittany and in Scotland, had given way to ritual and incantation by the seventeenth century.[20]

Under the influence of the Renaissance, with the reaffirmation of Greek and Roman values, an "easy death" once again came to be regarded as an ideal. This is reflected, for example, in Thomas More's *Utopia*, which depicts a perfect society in which voluntary euthanasia is officially sanctioned. Although it is uncertain whether More approved of euthanasia, the right to die rather than to endure prolonged suffering was proclaimed by many in the sixteenth and seventeenth centuries. Montaigne believed that "the voluntariest death is the fairest." [21] Francis Bacon insisted that doctors should help dying patients "to make a fair and easy passage from life." [22] John Donne argued in favor of suicide as a form of voluntary euthanasia. Nevertheless, he refrained from proposing rules or instances to justify the practice, because he felt that "the limits are obscure, and steepy and slippery and narrow, and every error deadly." [23]

The Renaissance dispelled many of the superstitions and misconceptions of the past. The scientific discoveries of this period, combined with an emphasis on the value of human life, gave rise to more effective measures for treating diseases. At the same time, however, efforts to keep patients alive often caused suffering which threatened to diminish the value of life. Bacon, Montaigne, and Donne were among the first to recognize this dilemma in the practice of modern medicine. By the end of the eighteenth century, members of the medical profession were also calling attention to their responsibility to make death as "natural" and as "human" as possible. In his *Oratio de Euthanasia*, in 1794, Paradys underscored the importance of the physician's duty to secure an easy death for his patients.

Throughout the nineteenth century, physicians continued

to emphasize the need to provide "natural" euthanasia. In 1826, Carl F. H. Marx delivered an oral thesis, entitled "Medical Euthanasia," which criticized doctors who treat diseases rather than patients and lose interest when they cannot cure. Marx insisted that the physician "is not expected to have a remedy for death but for the skillful alleviation of suffering and he should know how to apply it when all hope has departed." [24]

Most of those who argued in favor of euthanasia had only "natural," or passive, euthanasia in mind. They desired to aid nature in making death easy rather than to terminate life. In an address to the Maine Medical Association in 1889, Dr. Frank E. Hitchcock opposed active euthanasia but urged doctors to relieve the suffering of dying patients. Against changing the law to sanction passive euthanasia, he argued that "equity would regard the intent of the physician who humanely assists the patient in and out of his suffering." [25] Simeon E. Baldwin, president of the American Science Association in 1899, maintained that there is a natural right to a natural death.

There were also appeals for active euthanasia before the end of the nineteenth century. In an essay published by the Birmingham Speculative Club in 1870, S. D. Williams, Jr., insisted that it was the duty of the physician in cases of hopeless and painful illness "to destroy consciousness at once and put the sufferer to a quick and painless death." [26] He warned, however, that every effort should be made to prevent any possible abuse of this duty. By the end of the nineteenth century, a society had been organized in England to secure such a change in the law. Although the society attracted well-known supporters, it was ruled illegal and dissolved.

THE CONTEMPORARY PERIOD

The first significant appeal of the twentieth century for legalizing the practice of active euthanasia in England came in an address by Dr. C. E. Goddard before the Willesden and District Medical Society in 1901. In the United States, the first such bill was introduced in the Ohio legislature in 1906. It would have legalized voluntary euthanasia for adults of sound mind who are fatally hurt, terminally ill, or suffering extreme pain, but it was sent to a committee for study and was never passed. In 1912 a woman petitioned the New York State legislature to permit her physician to put her painlessly to death because she was suffering from an incurable disease and was in constant pain. This appeal also failed to secure legal sanctions for euthanasia.

Efforts to change the law, however, stimulated public controversy concerning mercy killing. Dr. Abraham Jacobi, president of the American Medical Association in 1912, warned that to yield to those who favored euthanasia "would make true what Plato said of the practice of medicine: 'it is no respectable calling.' " [27] On the other side of the issue, Dr. William J. Robinson claimed that euthanasia is fully justified for the incurably ill and an imperative duty for the hopelessly insane. Robinson argued that life is sacred only when it is pleasant, wanted, and bearable.

The issue continued to be discussed in the press in response to a number of controversial cases of mercy killing. In 1915 the question of euthanasia was posed by the death of the Bollinger baby. With the consent of the parents, Dr. H. J. Haiselden had refused to perform an operation that would have extended its life, because the child would have been radically deformed, partially paralyzed, and probably mentally abnormal. His choice was both praised and denounced, and he was finally expelled from the Chicago Medical Society. In response to this case, *The New Statesman* warned prophetically that if we grant the principle that doctors have the right to destroy life, we have no guarantee that they might not be swept off their feet someday by some pseudoeugenics which would involve widespread destruction of human life.

In 1920 the question of aiding suicide out of mercy was an issue in the case of *The People* v. *Frank C. Roberts* in Michigan. At the insistence of his wife, who suffered with multiple sclerosis and had attempted suicide, Roberts had prepared the glass of water and Paris green with which she had committed suicide. In what became a leading judicial decision on the subject, and one approved on appeal by the Supreme Court of Michigan, Roberts was convicted of willful murder and sentenced to life imprisonment at hard labor and in solitary confinement.

Other cases, however, met with less severity. In 1925, Dr. Harold E. Blazer was tried in Colorado for killing his daughter, an incurable invalid whom he had nursed for thirty-two years. When the jury was unable to reach a verdict, his case was dismissed. Several years later in Los Angeles, Ruth B. Weiner was freed by a jury before which she admitted having shot her sister who had begged to be killed. In 1933 a coroner's jury in Atlanta found that Allie Stephens, who had suffered for five or six years from cancer, died of natural causes rather than from the violent blow given at her request by a nephew.

In the State of New York, in 1938, a Nassau County grand jury refused to indict Harry C. Johnson for asphyxiating his wife, who had cancer and apparently wanted to die. The next year, Louis Greenfield was acquitted by a jury in the Bronx, New York City. He had been charged with first-degree manslaughter in the death of his seventeen-year-old son, who had been paralyzed and mentally retarded. After having read newspaper accounts of the Greenfield case, Louis Repouille chloroformed his thirteen-year-old son, who had been deformed and mute since birth and blind for five years. Repouille was tried and convicted of manslaughter in the second degree. Because the jury recommended clemency, a five to ten year sentence was imposed but was stayed, and he was placed on probation.

The question of mercy killing was also raised by cases in which the persons who had killed out of pity took their own lives. There were other cases in which patients suffering from incurable diseases took the matter into their own hands. The most widely publicized of these suicides was that of Charlotte Perkins Gilman, a noted American writer and the great-granddaughter of Lyman Beecher. In an article published in *The Forum* shortly before her death in 1935, she appealed for legislative changes to sanction euthanasia for those suffering incurable mental or physical illnesses.

A survey conducted by *Fortune* in 1937 reflects something of the climate of public opinion with regard to the practice of euthanasia.[28] In contrast with 40.5 percent who unconditionally rejected euthanasia for defective infants, 14.5 percent were undecided, and 45.0 percent approved its practice under the following conditions:

    13.9% – with the permission of the family
    23.3% – with the approval of a medical board
     7.8% – with the approval of a medical board and the
           permission of the family

In contrast with 47.5 percent who unconditionally rejected euthanasia for the incurably ill, 15.2 percent were undecided, and 37.3 percent approved its practice under these conditions:

    11.6% – with the permission of the patient
     4.2% – with the permission of the family

10.9% – with the approval of a medical board
1.7% – with the permission of the patient and the
family
8.9% – with the permission of the patient and/or the
family and approval of a medical board

Cases involving euthanasia also occurred in England, along with renewed efforts to legalize its practice. In one such case, which took place in Yorkshire in 1934, Mrs. May Brownhill murdered her son, Denis. He had been a helpless imbecile for thirty years and had demanded her constant care. Although the jury returned a verdict of "guilty," with the strongest recommendation of mercy, Mrs. Brownhill was sentenced to death. Two days later, however, she was reprieved, and in three months she was pardoned and released. Shortly thereafter, a similar case was tried in Manchester in which two sisters, charged with murdering their thirty-year-old imbecile brother, were found guilty but insane. In London in 1935, a twenty-two-year-old girl who was tried on the charge of murdering her insane mother was found not guilty, because the cause of death was ruled to have been pneumonia (even though the pneumonia was a direct result of the poison).

An important movement to gain legislative approval of euthanasia began in England with Dr. C. Killick Millard's presidential address before The Society of Medical Officers of Health in 1931. In this address, Dr. Millard described euthanasia as an elementary human right. In order to secure this right, he proposed a Voluntary Euthanasia Legislation Bill which included the following provisions:

1. An application for a euthanasia permit may be filed by a dying person stating that he has been informed by two medical practitioners that he is suffering from a fatal and incurable disease and that the process of death is likely to be protracted and painful.

2. The application must be attested by a magistrate and accompanied by two medical certificates.

3. The application and certificates must be examined and the patient and relative interviewed by a "euthanasia referee."

4. A court will then review the application, certificates, the testimony of the referee and any other representatives of the patient. It will then issue a permit to receive euthanasia to the applicant and a permit to administer euthanasia to a medical practitioner (or euthanisor).

5. The permit would be valid for a specified period within which the patient would determine if and when he wished to use it.[29]

The British Voluntary Euthanasia Legislation Society was founded in 1935 to promote this bill. Its supporters included Lord Moynihan, for years president of the Royal College of Surgeons and first president of the Voluntary Euthanasia Legislation Society, Dean W. R. Inge, Rev. R. W. Norwood, Professors Harold J. Laski and Julian S. Huxley, George Bernard Shaw, H. G. Wells, Sir W. Arbuthnot Lane, the Earl of Listowel, and Lord and Lady Denman. Their opponents were equally outstanding and represented a similar cross section of vocations. In 1936 they succeeded in defeating the bill in the House of Lords by a vote of thirty-five to fourteen.

Efforts to legalize euthanasia in America began again in 1937 with a bill introduced in the Nebraska legislature entitled the Voluntary Euthanasia Act. This bill was modeled on the English bill, but it differed in at least two important respects. In the first place, it would have granted euthanasia to any person who claimed to have an incurable and fatal disease, including those who were helpless and suffering the infirmities of old age. In the second place, it would have permitted the next of kin to make application on behalf of a mentally incompetent adult and a parent or guardian to make application on behalf of a minor whose condition was incurable or fatal. Like the English bill, the Voluntary Euthanasia Act would have granted legal immunity to the physician who performed euthanasia in accordance with its requirements.

In 1938 the Euthanasia Society of America was founded and began to campaign for legalizing euthanasia. The founder and first president of the new movement was Rev. Charles Francis Potter. Among the supporters of its program, opinions ranged from those who approved of euthanasia within conservative limits and with strict safeguards, to those whose approval extended to cases excluded in the proposed bills. Dr. Foster Kennedy, head of the Neurological Division of Bellevue Hospital, recommended "the release from living of those who should never have lived at all." [30] He subsequently retracted his arguments in favor of euthanasia for the incurably ill because of the danger of errors. The position of Dr. Alexis Carrel, a renowned research surgeon and Nobel laureate, was more radical: "Not only incurables, but kidnappers, murderers, habitual criminals of all kinds as well as the hopelessly insane, should be quietly and painlessly disposed of." [31]

Opponents of the measures proposed by the Euthanasia Society were equally outstanding and outspoken. Dr. Iago Galdston, executive secretary of the New York Academy of Medicine, argued that euthanasia was "contrary to the spirit and letter of medical ethics." [32] Dr. A. A. Brill, a noted psychiatrist, warned that "far from benefitting humanity mercy-killing would do incalculable harm." [33] Dr. Max Cutler, director of the tumor clinic of Michael Reese Hospital of Chicago, insisted that "we do not have the moral right even to consider any course except an effort to bring about the recovery of the patient." [34] "Even if it were legal for a doctor to take life," claimed Dr. Russell L. Haden, chief of the Department of Medicine at Cleveland

Clinic, "advances constantly being made in the science of medicine might make him regret it." [35]

Like its British counterpart, the Euthanasia Society of America was unsuccessful in its attempt to gain approval for its proposals. The Nebraska bill was referred to committee and was never acted upon further. An attempt to secure the passage of a similar bill in the New York legislature also failed. Efforts to establish the practice of euthanasia in Germany, however, took a radically different turn. The program that was established resulted from the philosophical and political orientation of Nazi Socialism.

The concept of *lebensunwerten Leben* (lives not worthy of life) provided the rationale for the Nazi practice of euthanasia. Coined by Karl Binding and elaborated by Binding and Hoche in *Die Freigabe der Vernichtung lebensunwerten Lebens* in 1920, this term referred to a patient's objective uselessness to the community. In contrast with the majority of English and American appeals for euthanasia, which were based on humanitarian regard for the suffering, Binding's argument was that useless, especially institutionalized idiots should be destroyed by the state in order to rid society of an unnecessary burden.[36] Although this idea was opposed by religious spokesmen, it had popular support in Germany. According to a poll conducted in 1920 by the psychiatrist Meltzer, 73 percent of the parents and guardians of mentally deficient children favored extermination of the latter. Furthermore, arguments for terminating *lebensunwerten Leben* appeared in German medical and legal literature of the period.[37]

Nazi Socialism was based on a philosophy that subordinated the individual to the community. Even before openly assuming power, the Nazis initiated propaganda efforts to undermine traditional values and to establish their utilitarian and racist ideology.[38] Eugenic measures were justified on this basis and were implemented with ruthless power.

They ran the gamut from the enforced "mercy deaths" initially for the mentally ill, and subsequently for the "useless eaters," through "special treatment" (extermination) for "inveterate German-haters" and for races declared to be inferior: the Poles, Russians, Jews, and Gypsies.[39]

It is interesting to note that legal reform measures to sanction euthanasia for the benefit of the patient were rejected because they were based on an individualistic social attitude.[40] Nevertheless, the extermination of the physically and socially unfit was practiced outside the law and uncensured by the government. In fact, this "euthanasia" was so openly accepted that it was referred to incidentally in a German medical journal in 1936. Following a directive signed by Hitler in 1939, a Nazi euthanasia program was initiated, and secret institutions were established to carry it out with efficiency and speed. Cooperating with this program as medical consultants were German doctors and professors of psychiatry from major universities. By the end of the war, they had "examined" and executed at least 275,000 people in special euthanasia centers. In many cases, the expenses were paid by unwilling relatives, and death certificates were falsified.[41]

One might conjecture that public opinion in America concerning euthanasia was fundamentally changed by the events in Germany during World War II. Such a conclusion, however, is not supported by surveys that were conducted in 1936 and 1939 and again in 1947 and 1950 by the American Institute of Public Opinion.

Responses in 1936 and in 1939 to the question: "Do you favor mercy deaths under government supervision for hopeless invalids?" [42]

Year	Yes	No	No Opinion
1936	38.64%	45.36%	16.0%
1939	41.40%	48.60%	10.0%

Responses in 1947 and 1950 to the question: "When a person has a disease that cannot be cured, do you think doctors should be allowed by law to end the patient's life by some painless means if the patient and the family request it?" [43]

Year	Yes	No	No Opinion
1947	37.0%	54.0%	9.0%
1950	43.0%	46.0%	11.0%

The similarity of responses to these polls suggests that the war and the disastrous Nazi "euthanasia" practices had little if any effect on the way in which Americans felt toward the practice and the legalization of voluntary euthanasia.

In 1945 the Euthanasia Society of America began a new campaign in New York to secure legislation to permit euthanasia. Its program was backed by 1,776 physicians and was supported by 54 eminent clergymen, including Dr. Henry Sloane Coffin, president of Union Theological Seminary, and Dr. Harry Emerson Fosdick, minister of Riverside Church in Manhattan. In the following year, 1,100 of the physicians who had endorsed this cause signed a petition to the state legislature in support of a bill which would provide that:

(1) Any sane person over twenty-one years old, suffering from an incurably painful and fatal disease, may petition a court of record for euthanasia, in a signed and attested document, with an affidavit from the attending physician that in his opinion the disease was incurable;

(2) The court shall appoint a commission of three, of whom at least two shall be physicians, to investigate all aspects of the case and to report back to the courts whether the patient understands the purpose of his petition and comes under the provisions of the act;

(3) Upon a favorable report by the commission the court shall grant the petition, and *if it is still wanted by the patient* euthanasia may be administered by a physician or any other person chosen by the patient or by the commission.[44]

The Euthanasia Society was not able to get this bill introduced in the New York legislature. Nevertheless, it continued its efforts with a petition signed by 379 Protestant and Jewish spokesmen in 1949 and with another petition signed by 2,000 voters in 1952.

An attempt by the British Euthanasia Society to secure favorable legislation for voluntary euthanasia in 1950 was quickly thwarted. This time it was no better prepared than its American counterpart, for it no longer had the benefit of highly placed peers who had spoken in its behalf in 1936. A petition was sent to the United Nations in 1952 to amend the Universal Declaration of Human Rights to include the right of incurable sufferers to voluntary euthanasia. In 1957 the Euthanasia Society of America sent a petition signed by 166 physicians to the New Jersey legislature. None of these measures, however, succeeded in gaining legal sanctions for euthanasia.

In spite of its failure to accomplish its primary objective, the American Euthanasia Society succeeded in calling attention to the problem of euthanasia and in attracting prominent supporters for its cause. Its advisory council included Dr. Walter C. Alvarez, Margaret Sanger, Robert Frost, and W. Somerset Maugham. The proposals of the Euthanasia Society also generated a distinguished opposition. The director of the National Institute of Health, Dr. R. E. Dyer, objected to its petition in 1947, claiming that "it is silly to talk about 'hopeless' [disease] in these times." [45] The presiding judge of the Archdiocesan Ecclesiastical Tribunal of New York, Msgr. Robert E. McCormick, termed the petition "Anti-God, un-American and a menace to

Veterans." [46] Denouncing the fifty-four clergymen who endorsed it, the general secretary of the American Council of Churches charged that "the modernistic clergy have made further departure from the eternal moral law." [47] Members of the General Convention of the Protestant Episcopal Church in the U.S.A., in 1952, categorically opposed legalizing the practice of euthanasia.

A series of cases involving mercy killing continued to call attention to the problem. Even though every attempt to sanction its practice met with strong opposition, laws against euthanasia were seldom enforced rigorously. In fact, relatively few cases were prosecuted. In those brought to trial, juries tended to take the circumstances into account in reaching their decisions.

In 1950 there were four noteworthy cases in which euthanasia was an issue. One case involved Carol Paight, a twenty-one-year-old college student in Connecticut, who killed her father after exploratory surgery had revealed that he had cancer. Miss Paight was charged with second-degree murder but was acquitted on the basis of temporary insanity. In another case, Harold A. Mohr was tried in Pennsylvania for the death of his brother, who was blind and had cancer. Even though Mohr pleaded temporary insanity, he was convicted of voluntary manslaughter. Because the jury recommended mercy, a relatively light sentence of three to five years in prison and a five-hundred-dollar fine was imposed. A third case, which occurred in Michigan, was that of Eugene Braunsdorf, a musician, who shot his twenty-nine-year-old deformed and retarded daughter and then attempted to commit suicide. He was accused of murder but was acquitted by reason of temporary insanity.

The case of Dr. Herman N. Sander in New Hampshire was especially significant, because it was the first case involving a medical doctor. Initially it appeared that this would be the test case for euthanasia. Dr. Sander was tried for having killed Mrs. Abbie Borrato, a patient who was dying with cancer. On December 4, 1949, Dr. Sander had stated in the hospital records that he had injected 10 cc. of air into her veins. According to the attending nurse, Mrs. Borrato died ten minutes later. Dr. Sander explained that he had acted out of pity, but the presiding judge declared that legally euthanasia could not be a factor in the trial. Nevertheless, the motive was the central issue in the public discussion surrounding the trial. It also seems to have been a primary factor in the jury's acquittal of Dr. Sander.

Mercy killings continued to take place throughout the country over the next twenty-five years. It is impossible, however, to determine the extent of the practice because of the tendency not to report and not to prosecute such cases. When they were brought to trial, the judicial system continued to treat with leniency those who had practiced euthanasia. A case that occurred in Maine in 1952 was exceptional in at least two respects. In the first place, the victim, who was killed by his father, Charles M. Collins, was not dying but was so violent that he was about to be sent to a state mental hospital. In the second place, the law was not applied with the leniency associated with cases of mercy killing, as Collins was found guilty and sentenced to life imprisonment.

There were other cases of euthanasia during this period which were somewhat more typical. In 1953, for example, William R. Jones was tried for having electrocuted his wife, an amputee and a diabetic, who was in constant pain. Jones was found guilty, but was sentenced to only one year and one day. The same year in New Jersey, Albert Sell was prosecuted for killing his five-year-old son, who was a victim of cerebral palsy. Sell was judged to be insane, placed in a mental institution and released after a year.

In *People* v. *Werner*, an Illinois case in 1958, the

defendant pleaded guilty to a charge of manslaughter for having suffocated his wife. She was suffering with rheumatoid arthritis and had begged to be killed. After testimony concerning her pain and his devotion to her, he was allowed to change his plea to not guilty and was acquitted. In another Illinois case in 1967, Robert Waskins, a twenty-two-year-old college student, was tried for having killed his mother. She was terminally ill with leukemia and suffering extreme pain when Robert entered her Chicago hospital room and shot her three times. Previously, she had attempted to commit suicide and had begged her son to kill her. Robert was acquitted on a plea of insanity and was released on the grounds that he was no longer insane.

In a similar case in New Jersey in 1973, Lester Zygmaniak was prosecuted for killing his brother in the Jersey Shore Medical Center. The brother had been paralyzed below the neck in a motorcycle accident and had begged to be killed. Lester was charged with first-degree murder but was acquitted on the basis of temporary insanity.

A second case involving a medical doctor was tried in New York in 1973. Dr. Vincent A. Montemarano, the chief surgical resident of the Nassau County Medical Center, had administered a lethal dose of potassium chloride to Eugene Bauer, a patient who was dying of throat cancer and was comatose. A nurse witnessed the injection, which Dr. Montemarano later stated was given for the patient's condition rather than to kill him. He was indicted on a charge of willful murder and found not guilty.

These cases indicate the flexibility of the judicial process when confronted with difficult moral problems. Nevertheless, such cases failed to come to terms with the fundamental question of a patient's right to die rather than to endure useless suffering. In spite of mounting concern over civil rights in general, the right to die with dignity received little attention and attracted few supporters. In fact, after efforts failed in 1950 and in 1957, there were no new initiatives to legalize euthanasia until 1969. Since then, numerous proposals have been offered to guarantee the principle of a dignified death. Unlike earlier proposals which sought to sanction active euthanasia, the new programs concentrated primarily on securing approval for passive euthanasia.

The concept of death with dignity, underlying recent legislative proposals on euthanasia, began to receive wide support as a result of a program sponsored by the Euthanasia Education Fund. This sister organization of the Euthanasia Society of America was founded in 1967 to disseminate information concerning the problem of euthanasia. In an effort to make it possible for individuals to request to die with dignity in the case of irreversible illness, the Euthanasia Education Fund prepared and distributed a formal request which has been called a "living will." On the basis of the principle that a person has a right to refuse medical care, it makes the following petition:

> If there is no reasonable expectation of my recovery from physical or mental disability, I, _____, request that I be allowed to die and not be kept alive by artificial means or heroic measures.

This document, when signed and witnessed, is like a will which is intended to be a testament of a patient's wishes when he is no longer able to take part in medical decisions.

Efforts to legalize euthanasia in Great Britain were renewed in 1969 with a bill introduced in the House of Lords. Like the "living will," the Voluntary Euthanasia Act of 1969 would allow a person to sign a declaration beforehand requesting euthanasia in the case of terminal illness. This declaration would require that no active steps be taken to prolong life or to restore consciousness when a person's condition becomes incurable and is expected to cause severe distress or to make him incapable of rational existence. According to the bill, the declaration would go into effect thirty days after it was completed and would be renewable on a three-year basis for life.

The procedures of the Voluntary Euthanasia Act were designed both to meet objections to the extensive formalities required by other bills and to provide protection against mistakes and abuse. It authorized doctors to perform euthanasia on any patient whose declaration was in effect and who had been certified by two physicians as having an "irremediable condition." In the case of a mentally competent patient, the bill required that the physician determine that the declaration and all the steps to be taken were in accordance with his wishes. Legal immunity and the presumption of good faith were provided for doctors and nurses who practice euthanasia in accordance with these provisions. The objections that this bill failed to meet were not procedural but fundamental objections to the principle of euthanasia. Thus, on a second reading, it was defeated by a vote of 61 to 40. In response to an attempt to reintroduce it in 1970, it was voted down again with a chorus of "No's."

Legislative proposals to guarantee the principle of death with dignity have also been introduced in the United States. In 1969 a bill was proposed in the Florida legislature to amend the Declaration of Human Rights to include the right to die with dignity. When the bill failed to be reported out of committee, it was reintroduced as a statute to sanction passive euthanasia. Like the British bill, it would require a document, to be executed like a will, declaring a person's wish not to have his life prolonged beyond the point of meaningful existence.

Bills that are similar to the Florida bill in many respects have been introduced in a number of states, including Idaho, Montana, Oregon, West Virginia, and Wisconsin. There are at least two important points at which there are differences. In the first place, proposals in some states would require that the request be made only by a competent adult. Other proposals would permit the request to be made on behalf of a minor by the parents or guardian and on behalf of an incompetent patient by a spouse or the next of kin. In the second place, some of the bills would authorize the cessation of only extraordinary, artificial, or heroic measures to prolong life. Other bills would permit the discontinuation of all measures to prolong life. All the proposals, however, would require a witnessed document and would provide procedure for revoking the request. They all would require medical certification that the patient's condition was hopeless and would grant immunity to doctors who honor the patient's request.

Legislative proposals such as these are only first steps toward solving the problem of suffering in terminal medical care. Our society has yet to make significant progress in terms of confronting and resolving this question in a responsible manner. There is, however, a growing interest in the problem, which is expressed both in the popular media and in professional circles. This is true of the medical profession in particular, and doctors are becoming more involved in efforts to establish new standards of medical care for the suffering and dying. One of the bills calling for death with dignity in Florida, for example, was introduced by W. W. Sackett, Jr., a medical doctor and a member of the Florida legislature.

In his presidential address before the Association of American Physicians in 1969, Dr. Robert H. Williams surveyed the attitudes and practices of American doctors concerning euthanasia and concluded that a majority favored and practice passive euthanasia. In an editorial in 1970, Dr. Alister Brass, senior editor of the *Journal of the American Medical Association*, indicated that euthanasia is being practiced to a wide extent. He called for doctors to become involved in the debate on the problem. The New York Medical Association adopted a resolution in 1973 declaring active euthanasia to be outside the province of the physician but affirming the patient's right to die with dignity. The same year, the American Medical Association reiterated its opposition to mercy killing but acknowledged the dying patient's right to refuse extraordinary measures to keep him alive.

It would be interesting to have an accurate reading of public opinion concerning the morality of euthanasia and with regard to legalizing its practice. Unfortunately, however, there are conflicts in the data that are available. In response to a Louis Harris survey in 1973, 62 percent favored (and 38 percent opposed) sanctioning passive euthanasia, while 37 percent favored (and 53 percent opposed) sanctioning active euthanasia.[48] Since the results of this report correspond with earlier surveys, one might conclude that there has been no significant change in public attitudes toward euthanasia over the last forty years. A somewhat different picture, however, was reflected in a Gallup survey in 1973. In response to the same question asked in surveys in 1947 and 1950, 53 percent agreed that doctors should be allowed by law to end a patient's life when he cannot be cured and when the patient and the family request it.[49] This would indicate an important change in public approval of active euthanasia.

Clearly, the controversy over euthanasia cannot be easily resolved. The medical, legal, and moral issues are far too complex, and opinions are too deeply divided to expect a general consensus to emerge as a basis for new standards for terminal medical practice. Many people prefer to rely on the inherent flexibility of our legal system in dealing with specific cases rather than to change the law governing the practice of medicine. This approach to the problem is inadequate in at least two respects. In the first place, specific instances involving moral application of legal norms fail to come to terms with fundamental issues in such a way as to establish legal precedents for other cases. Thus, they do not guarantee that similar cases will be treated with the same moral insight. In the second place, these cases do not provide legal and moral guidance for doctors who are confronted with the problem of hopeless suffering in the context of life and death decisions.

In the final analysis, the same moral insight that is required for refined moral judgments in specific cases is necessary in order to formulate new and responsible standards for the practice of medicine. The purpose of the following chapters is to analyze arguments for and against the morality of euthanasia and to examine the medical and the legal dimensions of this question. On this basis, moral guidelines are proposed for terminal medical care and for legal norms relative to the practice of euthanasia.

2
EUTHANASIA:
PRO AND CON

A review of the literature on euthanasia, especially in the popular press, gives one the impression of a somewhat unstructured and unresolved public debate on the question. Specific cases of mercy killing generate reactions of approval and disapproval. Arguments for death with dignity inspired by instances of hopeless suffering are countered by arguments warning of the dangerous consequences of assuming the right to take life. Legislative proposals to sanction euthanasia are met with rebuttal by those who oppose. In its broadest terms, this debate is concerned with the morally proper medical treatment for suffering and dying patients and with the legal measures by which this can be kept secured and protected.

There are at least three principal reasons that this controversy has remained unsolved for so long. In the first place, the medical and legal dimensions of the question of euthanasia are extremely complex. In the second place, there are fundamental conflicts of values which are implicit, if not explicit, in the arguments on both sides of the issue. In short, opinions are too diverse and too insufficiently informed to make possible the consensus necessary for resolving the problem. In the third place, death is such a taboo in our society that it is feared and denied. Death and the threat of death tend to undermine and to destroy our values rather than to provide perspectives from which they can be ordered.

A survey of the history of euthanasia reveals that its practice has been sanctioned or censured in the past on the basis of the beliefs, values, and superstitions that have prevailed in various cultures. Similarly, an analysis of the current controversy over euthanasia should disclose the basic issues in question and the areas of disagreement that block efforts to reach workable and satisfactory solutions. Furthermore, a study of medical practices in cases involving hopeless suffering and a study of legal practices in cases involving mercy killing should reveal the ways in which the values and ethical principles of our culture are ordered and interpreted.

The purpose of this chapter is to summarize and to analyze the principal arguments for and against euthanasia. The basic presupposition underlying this study is that the controversy can be resolved and that responsible policies for dealing with the problem of hopeless suffering can be worked out. This will require a thorough understanding of the medical, legal, social, and psychological dimensions of the question. It will also require an appropriate ordering of the complementary and the conflicting moral values and ethical principles that serve as the basis of medical ethics and legal norms.

THE LOGIC OF MORAL DISCOURSE

To get to the basic issues involved in the debate over euthanasia, it is necessary to take into account the nature of moral discourse in general. As in any serious controversy, judgments are made and opinions are expressed on various levels of moral significance. Henry David Aiken suggests that there are at least four distinct levels of moral discourse: (1) the "expressive-evocative" level; (2) the "moral" level; (3) the "ethical" level; and (4) the "post-ethical" level.[1] Aiken explains the use of moral language and the role of judgments in each of these levels. His typology serves as an instructive tool for analyzing the conflicting arguments over euthanasia. It also serves to explain the basis and function of professional medical ethics and of legal norms relative to this question.

On the "expressive-evocative" level, moral discourse consists of spontaneous and unreflective expressions, such as emotional responses of praise or blame. Such expressions serve to vent emotions and to reflect personal feelings that do not call for proof or justification. Opposite expressions simply indicate basically different emotional reactions. To inquire concerning which is correct is to move to another level of discourse.

Most of our moral deliberations and decisions take place on the "moral" level. Discourse on this level is essentially practical, concerned primarily with problems of conduct. It has to do with the question, "What ought I do in this situation?" In answering this question and in justifying decisions or actions, moral discourse involves factual appraisals of the available means and of the consequences of various alternatives. Moral discourse also appeals to explicitly moral rules and procedures in order to establish the relevance of such appraisals. A good reason or a valid justification for a given decision is, in Aiken's terms, one that is determined by socially affirmed rules or codes.

Moral discourse proceeds to the "ethical" level when either the validity or the authority of the rules of morality is challenged. This may occur when there are conflicting rules. It also may happen when accepted standards of conduct cause general inconvenience or suffering and when they run counter to human needs or desires. Unlike "moral" discourse, which has to do with specific problems of conduct, "ethical" discourse has to do with ordering and correcting the rules and standards of morality. In contrast with moral rules, which prescribe what to do in specific cases, ethical principles and rules serve as the basis for appraising moral rules. They include such principles as justice (or fair treatment) and humanity (or least suffering), which are self-justifying; that is, they establish what constitutes ethical reason.

Discourse on the "post-ethical" level has to do with questions concerning the validity of ethical principles. To answer these questions, it is necessary to go beyond the limits of moral discourse altogether. In the final analysis, the authority and the validity of ethical principles and moral norms is dependent upon their affirmation. The metaphysical or theological basis of such commitments is therefore the subject of post-ethical discourse. The way in which human existence is understood in relation to the ultimate center or centers of value has an important bearing on the meaning and order of ethical principles. Moral discourse on the post-ethical level provides the rationale for fundamental ethical principles and engages in critical appraisals of conflicting ethical systems.

THE CONTROVERSY OVER EUTHANASIA

In the debate over euthanasia, discussion does not simply begin at one level of moral discourse and proceed to higher levels as the controversy becomes more involved. Furthermore, there is no common logic of moral discourse in this debate. Moral norms that are treated as absolutes in one argument are regarded simply as "rules of thumb" in another. Ethical values that are interpreted by some as ends or goals are understood by others as duties or commands. Since the arguments are essentially practical in intent, they frequently shift from one level to another in a pragmatic rather than in a logical manner. They appeal not only to relatively objective rules or principles but also to subjective feelings or inclinations in order to clinch their cases.

The shifts between the various levels of discourse in the arguments on both sides of the question often obscure the essential issues in question. Conclusions are often affirmed on the basis of tacit assumptions of agreement with regard to the meaning and order of moral norms and ethical values when, in fact, there is no such consensus. An analysis of the arguments over euthanasia in terms of the levels of moral discourse exposes basic disagreements concerning appropriate moral standards for terminal medical care. It also reveals fundamental differences of opinion with regard to the ethical principles underlying such standards.

Initial responses to specific cases in which suffering is prolonged or intensified by efforts to prolong life often are verbalized on a purely "expressive" level. Arguments for and against euthanasia in such cases give rise to similarly spontaneous reactions. These emotional, reflex responses are essentially impulsive expressions of approval or disapproval. They are usually based on unexamined commitments, alternatives, and consequences. In the course of the debate over euthanasia, confusion and misunderstandings have frequently resulted from conclusions hastily drawn from these initial responses.

When there is an attempt to justify or to refute these reactions, the moral argument moves to a higher level. This is not to say, however, that emotional or evocative language ceases to be employed. Most of the arguments on euthanasia invite emotional response in support of their conclusions. These emotive appeals attempt to foster a unanimity of opinions and attitudes with regard to moral obligations and ethical principles. They also tend to gloss over significant factual and moral questions.

The debate over euthanasia takes place primarily on the moral and ethical levels. Although it can be understood and resolved only in the context of current medical technology and its consequences, it is essentially a moral controversy. It involves such moral questions as: Should life be preserved as long as technically possible? Are there circumstances in which life should be terminated? Should patients who are suffering and dying be allowed to die by withdrawing or failing to employ life-sustaining procedures? Should their lives be taken by death-dealing narcotics? Should such steps be taken only at the request of the patient or in consultation with his family and his doctors?

The controversy over euthanasia is also concerned with the adequacy and the validity of the traditional moral rules or standards of medical practice. Implicit, if not explicit, in the various arguments on both sides of the question are basic ethical values and principles. These include such principles as the sanctity of life, the right to live, human dignity, personal autonomy, justice, and least suffering. It is with reference to these ethical values that the moral standards of medical practice are criticized or defended. It is also on this basis that new standards of terminal medical care are proposed.

The way in which ethical values are interpreted and applied in moral norms is contingent upon changing historical and cultural situations. They are flexible in relation to a broad range of human capacities, needs, and institutions. In "hard cases," however, when fundamental human needs conflict and when the claims of the individual cut across those of society, difficult choices often must be made among ethical principles, all of which are right. In relatively closed societies, religious or political ideology serves as the basis on which such decisions are made. In Western culture,

Christianity once defined the meaning and order of ethical principles. With the secularization of our society, however, ethical values have tended to become autonomous. There is no longer a common commitment with reference to which the relative value of competing ideals can be determined.

It is in the context of this crisis of values that the controversy over euthanasia must be understood. Conflicting arguments with regard to the validity of traditional moral standards of medical practice result from fundamentally different interpretations of ethical values. Even when there seems to be a common commitment to a given principle, there are sometimes important differences of opinion. The value of life, for example, is affirmed both by those who favor euthanasia and by those who oppose its practice. The meaning of "life," however, is interpreted differently. Advocates of euthanasia emphasize the quality of life over its quantity and insist that the value of life is destroyed when it is accompanied by severe restrictions or suffering. Opponents of euthanasia emphasize the sanctity of life *per se* and claim that life always has value, regardless of its quality.

In the final analysis, concrete decisions and actions in the context of specific cases cut through all the ambiguities of apparently conflicting alternatives, consequences, and obligations. This occurs when a suffering patient asks to die, when a member of his family requests that efforts to prolong his life be stopped, or when a doctor orders an end to life-sustaining treatment or administers a death-dealing narcotic. It also occurs when a district attorney fails to prosecute or a jury refuses to convict someone who has practiced euthanasia. Strictly speaking, these decisions and actions transcend the limits of moral discourse altogether. They momentarily bring moral deliberation to a halt by cutting through the complexities and by positing answers. These *ad hoc* solutions to the problems of caring for the suffering and dying, however, become subject to moral appraisal. They can be explained and evaluated on both the moral and the ethical levels of moral discourse.

THE PRINCIPAL ARGUMENTS

There are two distinct, although closely related, issues involved in the controversy over euthanasia. The first is the question of the morality of various forms of euthanasia. The second question has to do with legalizing the practice of euthanasia. Arguments against euthanasia generally appeal first to prevailing professional and legal standards of medical practice. They then appeal to basic ethical principles in order to validate these moral norms forbidding euthanasia. Arguments favoring euthanasia usually begin by appealing directly to ethical values in order to challenge the validity of current standards of medical practice and to sanction the practice of euthanasia.

Prevailing standards of medical practice serve to protect a number of ethical values and reflect the priority usually assigned to these principles. In the "Principles of Medical Ethics" of the American Medical Association, for example, the medical profession is said to be dedicated "to the alleviation of suffering, the enhancement and prolongation of life, and to the destinies of humanity." [2] In difficult cases in which all these values cannot be achieved, decisions have to be made with regard to which of these values takes precedence. The legal system is more specific than professional medical ethics. It protects the right to life by enacting laws against homicide, and at the same time it acknowledges the priority of other values by sanctioning certain forms of "justifiable" homicide. Nevertheless, when, under the legal system, suicide is condemned and homicide at the request of the victim or in order to relieve suffering is

equated with murder, the legal system places the value of
life over the values of personal autonomy and least suffering.

The validity of these moral-level rules and standards
remains unchallenged so long as their requirements are
compatible with the accepted ethical principles and values.
Their adequacy for determining proper medical practice is
not questioned as long as the way in which basic values are
ordered is consistent with human needs. Arguments in
favor of euthanasia, however, challenge the relevance of
these moral standards to the needs of the terminally ill, the
fatally injured, and the severely abnormal. This challenge
takes the form of an "ethical criticism" both of medical
practices that prolong life after hope of recovery has been
abandoned and of legal norms that censure the practice of
euthanasia.

Proposals to sanction the practice of euthanasia are based
on essentially different conceptions of the order and priority
of ethical values. There are five basic principles to which
appeals are made for the practice of euthanasia. In the first
place, the dignity of life is said to be superior to the value of
life *per se*. This claim serves as the basis of a variety of
arguments. The belief that man should have the right to die
with dignity, just as he should have the right to live with
dignity, is expressed in the "living wills" sponsored by the
Euthanasia Education Fund. A number of legislative proposals have been made to guarantee the right to die with
dignity.

In the second place, it is often argued that when a patient
is suffering and incurable, the physician's responsibility to
relieve suffering is more important than his responsibility to
prolong life. Many concur with Dr. Frank J. Ayd that,
"when death is imminent and inevitable, it is neither
scientific nor humane to use artificial life-sustainers to
protect the life of a patient. Instead, when realistic hope of
recovery has evaporated, it is right to choose only ordinary

means to sustain his life and it is the duty of the doctor to provide palliative care." [3] Others approve of more direct measures of preventing suffering and agree with Glanville Williams that "a man is entitled to demand the release of death from hopeless and helpless pain, and a physician who gives this release is entitled to moral and legal absolution for his act." [4]

The principle of autonomy, or the right to be at liberty, is a third value which is often given precedence over the value of life which is radically restricted. Joseph Fletcher, for instance, insists that "to prolong life uselessly, while the personal qualities of freedom, knowledge, self-possession and control, and responsibility are sacrificed, is to attack the moral status of a person, to deny morality, and to submit to fatality." [5] Drs. Edgar E. Filbey and Kenneth E. Reed emphasize the importance of this value. They argue that the doctor, the pastor, and the chaplain are responsible for keeping the moral and ethical considerations in the forefront in terminal decisions. They insist, however, that "the onus of the decision belongs to the patient and those closest to him." [6]

In the fourth place, the principle of justice, or fair treatment, is cited in at least two ways as an important reason for permitting the practice of euthanasia. On the one hand, it is frequently argued that laws should be amended in fairness to suffering patients, because legal requirements tend to cause their suffering to be prolonged unnecessarily. It is claimed that while an easy death is secretly granted to some, it is denied to many others. Legalizing the practice of euthanasia would make it available for all. On the other hand, appeals on the grounds of the principle of justice are sometimes based on the claim that euthanasia should be permitted out of consideration for those other than the patient. Some claim that in fairness to doctors, who believe that the relief of suffering is one of their principal duties, the risk of being accused of breaking the law in order to fulfill this obligation should be removed. The needs and the rights of the families of the hopelessly ill and deformed are also said to justify the practice of euthanasia, since it is unfair to require of them the financial and emotional expense of prolonged and useless therapy.

A fifth principle affirmed in some of the arguments for modifying current medical practices of prolonging life and for changing laws against euthanasia is the principle of utility. On the basis of this principle, life is understood to be of value not as an end in itself but in terms of its usefulness as a means to the ends prescribed by society. The practice of euthanasia therefore is justified in certain circumstances, such as those involving the hopelessly ill and mental degeneratives, when treatment places a useless burden on society.

Euthanasia is altogether unacceptable when life is understood solely as an end in itself with priority over other values. When life is understood to be only a means to other ends, all forms of euthanasia may be advocated. Sometimes, however, certain forms that are likely to raise objections are eliminated from proposed reforms for the sake of expediency. In most of the proposals with regard to appropriate medical practices and legal norms relative to cases in which there is no hope of recovery, there is an attempt to preserve a number of ethical values and moral rights. Active euthanasia is frequently opposed, for example, because of the value of life itself. At the same time, however, passive euthanasia may be favored on the basis of other values, such as least suffering. Furthermore, voluntary euthanasia is often advocated over involuntary euthanasia, because the will or freedom of the individual is given precedence both over the value of life and over the needs or desires of family or society.

Although basic ethical principles are implicit in all the

arguments concerning euthanasia, some of the arguments do not proceed beyond the moral level of discourse. Those who oppose the practice of euthanasia often defend their positions simply by appealing to customary rules and procedures. They frequently cite the doctor's pledge in the Hippocratic Oath:

> I will use treatment to help the sick according to my ability and judgment, but never with a view to injury and wrong-doing. Neither will I administer a poison to anybody when asked to do so, nor will I suggest such a course.[7]

Apparently without realizing that conventional moral norms for medical care have been challenged, those who argue against euthanasia continue to claim that the ethics of the medical profession forbid the physician to take life. Dr. Phillips Frohman, for example, insists that "the preservation of human life is not only the primary but the all-encompassing general law underlying the order of the physician." [8]

Arguments on this level deal not only with strictly moral questions but also with empirical questions of terminal medical care. They express fundamentally different interpretations of medical problems of treating suffering patients and of the consequences of the various alternatives. Many who oppose the practice of euthanasia insist that dying patients continue to cling to life regardless of the circumstances and would not avail themselves of an early and easy death. The claims that euthanasia should be practiced in order to relieve their suffering are rejected as exaggerated. It is often argued that there is, indeed, no place for unbearable pain in modern medicine. It is also argued that doctors can and do make mistakes in diagnosis and prognosis that would result in unnecessary loss of life if euthanasia were permitted. Furthermore, the terms "hopeless" and "incurable" are said to be outmoded medical concepts. Because apparently incurable conditions may someday be

cured by a new medical breakthrough, it is concluded that
life should be prolonged as long as possible.

Those who argue in favor of the practice of euthanasia
insist that, because of the improvements in medical sci-
ences, the prolongation of life often becomes the prolongation of dying. They conclude that when death is inevitable
and efforts to prolong life cause suffering, doctors should
hasten death for the benefit of the patient. The argument
that life should be preserved as long as possible, because a
cure might be found, is rejected by the claim that any new
cure would be of no benefit for the patient for whom
euthanasia would be a consideration.

In addition to these factual disagreements relative to the
practice of euthanasia, there are similar differences of
opinion with regard to legalizing euthanasia. Opponents of
euthanasia emphasize the difficulties and the negative
consequences which, they claim, would result if euthanasia
were legalized. In the first place, they insist that it would
be virtually impossible to determine whether a patient
whose mind is weakened by narcotics and pain really wants
to die. They point out that such a patient would not be able
to make an informed decision. In the second place, they
argue that to permit euthanasia would require families to
make life and death decisions when they are least able
emotionally. In the third place, they warn that legal
sanctions for euthanasia would expand the power and
responsibility of the physicians, which are already almost
unbearably great. In the fourth place, they claim that the
practice of euthanasia would weaken medical research by
taking away the incentives to find cures for painful diseases.
Finally, it is argued that if the public once came to think
that their doctors might exchange the role of preserver for
that of destroyer, their suffering in anxiety would far
outweigh that now attributable to the unnecessary prolonging of life.

Many who approve of limited forms of euthanasia have misgivings about legalizing its practice in any form. They too fear that the benefit to a few would be outweighed by the threat to many others. With those who oppose euthanasia altogether, they argue that, since there can be no adequate safeguards, the practice would be open to serious abuse. Yale Kamisar, for instance, issues the following warning:

> Miss Voluntary Euthanasia is not likely to be going it alone for very long. Many of her admirers . . . would be neither surprised nor distressed to see her joined by Miss Euthanatize the Congenital Idiots and Miss Euthanatize the Permanently Insane and Miss Euthanatize the Senile Dementia. And these lasses—whether or not they themselves constitute a "parade of horrors"—certainly make excellent majorettes for such a parade.[9]

The practice of euthanasia in Nazi Germany is often cited in order to underscore this danger.

Those who not only approve of the practice of euthanasia but also favor legislative changes to sanction it discount such arguments. They in turn call attention to the negative consequences of the failure to legalize euthanasia. In the first place, they claim that since a doctor has to relieve suffering by measures that often hasten death, he runs the risk of being accused of breaking the law. In the second place, they emphasize the fact that euthanasia is already practiced secretly. They point out that the doctor usually has to take full responsibility, for he cannot consult with other physicians and can rarely ask for the consent of the patient or of relatives. Furthermore, they insist that, if euthanasia were legalized, its practice could be supervised, and both patients and doctors would be better protected. In the third place, the few cases of euthanasia that are brought to trial, the frequent acquittals, and the lenient sentences given to those found guilty are often cited as indications of the need for changes in the law. The discrepancies between the law in theory and the law in practice are said to undermine its effectiveness. Furthermore, as Helen Silving points out, "the system prevailing at the present does not afford equality of treatment of mercy killer." [10]

In order to proceed toward relevant and satisfactory solutions to the problem of suffering in terminal medical care, it is necessary to come to terms with these conflicting arguments which arise on the moral level of discourse concerning euthanasia. This will require an examination of the medical problems and alternatives in the treatment of the severely deformed, the fatally injured, and the incurably ill. It will also require a study of legal norms relative to the practice of euthanasia and an analysis of the way in which the law operates in the context of specific cases involving active and passive euthanasia. In the last analysis, however, in order to resolve the moral controversy over euthanasia, it is necessary to reconcile basic disagreements on the ethical level of discourse with regard to fundamental norms and values that should be preserved as a basis for moral and legal standards for the practice of medicine.

3
CONFLICTING RELIGIOUS VIEWS

The question of euthanasia has received much less attention in Christian ethics than other moral problems of medical practice, such as birth control, abortion, and organ transplants. Nevertheless, leading Roman Catholic and Protestant theologians have addressed this question. Furthermore, it is beginning to receive more attention in theological circles as the problems of caring for the suffering and dying become more acute. This chapter delineates a cross section of the positions in theological ethics with regard to the morality of euthanasia. It analyzes various underlying theological orientations and ethical methodologies in order to explain the conflicting interpretations of the requirements of Christian medical ethics. It endeavors to provide a perspective from which this controversy can be understood and the problem of euthanasia can be resolved.

THEOLOGY AND ETHICS

In any interpretation of Christian medical ethics there are central moral norms such as the requirement to preserve life, to relieve pain, and to care for the dying. There are also basic ethical principles, including the will of God, natural law, the commandment to love, the value of life, and the dignity of persons. The ways in which these moral requirements and ethical responsibilities are understood are determined by even more fundamental theological presuppositions. These assumptions must be taken into account in order to understand conclusions that are expressed in terms of moral values and in moral judgments and decisions.

In response to questions of medical ethics, Roman Catholic theologians usually begin with the requirements of natural law. Many philosophers and theologians within this tradition have criticized extremely rationalistic conceptions of natural law and legalistic interpretations of its moral-level norms. Nevertheless, the Catholic Church applies a strict natural law theory and derives absolute requirements in dealing with the problem of euthanasia. To understand these conclusions, it is important to recognize their premises on the post-ethical and ethical levels.

— The underlying principle of natural law is that good is to be done and evil is to be avoided. The first precept that man discerns requires that he preserve his life and health. This is one of the universal requirements of natural law which is known intuitively. On the basis of universal principles, practical reason deduces more specific, secondary principles. The farther reason proceeds from the basic moral axioms to a particular conclusion, the greater the possibility of exceptions and the danger of errors. However, through the "republication" of natural law in revelation and in the teachings of the church, secondary principles are given definitive interpretations.

— Roman Catholic moral philosophy interprets the principles of natural law and delineates two distinct types of moral requirements. Negative natural law principles prohibit actions that are intrinsically evil and actions that are evil because of the attending circumstances. Affirmative natural law principles prescribe that certain morally good acts be done. The former are based on the primary obligation to avoid evil, and they permit no exceptions. The latter are based on the fundamental responsibility to do good. These permit reasonable and proportionate limits, for although good ends never justify immoral means, morally evil ends may serve to justify the omission of good means. The principle of double effect provides the following criteria for determining when an action may be performed for the sake of a good effect in spite of a concomitant evil effect. In the first place, the action in question must be good in itself, or at least morally indifferent. In the second place, it must be the only means to the desired end. In the third place, only the good effect may be intended directly. In the fourth place, the good may not be produced by means of an evil effect. Finally, there must be a due proportion between the good, which is directly intended, and the evil, which is only permitted. This judgment is often quite difficult and must be made by prudent and conscientious men in the context of each case.

This orientation is the source of many of the standards that are outlined in Catholic texts on medical ethics. Disagreements among theologians on such questions as abortion and birth control reflect different conceptions of natural law and conflicting interpretations of its requirements. In various areas, absolute norms that are based on rationalistic understanding of natural law theory are being called into question. Nevertheless, the position of the Catholic Church with regard to the question of euthanasia is derived from a strict interpretation of natural law.

Among Protestant theologians, there are conflicting conclusions with regard to the morality of euthanasia. The positions of Karl Barth, Dietrich Bonhoeffer, Joseph Fletcher, and Paul Ramsey serve to illustrate significantly different approaches to this question. These differences stem from fundamentally different conceptions of Christian ethics, in general. Although the influence of natural law theory is evident in each of their discussions of euthanasia, they differ in their appraisals of this tradition. Bonhoeffer and Ramsey reinterpret and apply the insights of natural law. Barth and Fletcher, however, reject this theory as a basis for Christian ethics.

Karl Barth deals with the question of euthanasia on the moral level of theological ethics in relation to the command of God. His interpretation of this command is based on fundamental theological affirmations. This is indicative of his understanding of Christian ethics as a part of dogmatics rather than as an independent science. Barth's emphasis on Jesus Christ as the criterion of Christian ethics determines his rejection of natural law. This emphasis is central in his interpretation of the command of God as it is directed to man in the particular spheres of creation, reconciliation, and redemption. Although its content varies according to the sphere in which it is issued, Barth insists that there is only one command. The purpose of this command is always man's sanctification. This sanctifying claim, according to Barth, is the basis of an ethic of grace and freedom.

It is in his analysis of the command of God as "an imperative summons to freedom for human existence" [1] that Barth examines the problem of euthanasia. This command is said to require respect and protection for human life. On the one hand, Barth describes the obligation to protect life as a "direction for service" rather than as an absolute law or principle. Underlying this interpretation is his conception of Christian ethics as an ethics of obedience to the concrete command of God as it is addressed anew to men in each situation. On the other hand, however, in his explanation of the command to protect life in relation to the question of euthanasia, Barth claims that there are some acts which cannot be performed or justified in any situation, because they can never really seem to be commanded.

In contrast with Barth, Dietrich Bonhoeffer recognized the importance of natural law as a basis for resolving moral problems. Unlike traditional Roman Catholic moral philosophy, however, he interprets this theory from a Christological perspective. Bonhoeffer insists that it is only in its relation to Christ that the "natural" is recognized as "the form of life preserved by God for the fallen world and directed towards justification, redemption and renewal." [2] It is in relation to the natural right to life and the duty to preserve life that Bonhoeffer deals with the question of euthanasia.

Joseph Fletcher questions the validity of the absolute and universal principle requirements of natural law. His conclusions with regard to euthanasia are based instead on the requirements of love in relation to the needs of dying patients. His situational or contextual approach to decisions on the moral level is said to presuppose a theological positivism which "posits" or affirms faith in God as its basis. This faith determines its highest good, i.e., *agapē*. In addition to the commandment to love, there are three presuppositions or working principles in Fletcher's situation ethics: pragmatism, relativism, and personalism.

Fletcher's position on euthanasia can best be understood in relation to these presuppositions. As a personalist, he challenges the vitalism and naturalistic determinism of conventional medical ethics. He replaces these values with the personal values of human dignity, self-possession, and freedom of choice. Like the physicians, Fletcher is pragmatic in his approach to specific cases, but he is more concerned with personality than with biology. He is interested in the dying patient as a person rather than as a terminal case. Because he holds all moral norms to be relative to the requirements of love, he permits no "practice rules" for medical care. In the last analysis, he calls for moral response and responsibility and insists that "even the most revered principles may be thrown aside if they conflict in any concrete case with love." [3]

Paul Ramsey discusses the question of euthanasia on the moral level of Christian normative ethics in relation to two obligations: the duty to "save life" and the duty to "care for the dying." He interprets these responsibilities as "practice rules" of Christian ethics and as "faithfulness-claims" which all patients place on those who are entrusted with their care. In his delineation of the requirements of these generic duties, Ramsey defines the moral limits of the physician's duty to heal and to save life. He also underscores the importance of care and comfort for those who are dying. Finally, in relation to morally relevant features of patients and of practices, he examines the possible qualifications of the "categorical imperative: never abandon care." [4]

Underlying Ramsey's approach to specific moral problems is his conception of Christian ethics as an ethics of convenant loyalty. The Christian is said to begin with the requirements of love in response to the multiple needs and claims of his neighbors. This does not lead to an ethics of deeds only. According to Ramsey, there are faithfulness-claims which are comprehended in appropriate principles or canons of loyalty. There are also principles which express what love requires as a practice. In some cases, practice-oriented principles correspond with person-centered principles. Unlike canons of loyalty, however, practice rules have utilitarian justification. Consequently, the necessary qualification of one may not always be applicable to the other. In relation to the question of euthanasia, it is interesting to note that Ramsey cautiously suggests that his qualifications of the faithfulness-claim to care for the dying can also be made of this obligation as a rule of practice governing medical care.

The theological orientation and ethical methodologies

with which each theologian deals with the question of euthanasia determine his conception of the moral issues that are involved. They also determine the way in which he resolves the problems that he finds to be crucial. Consequently, much of the controversy over euthanasia in theological ethics can be explained in terms of conflicting theological and methodological presuppositions. These differences must be taken into account in an analysis of the various arguments on the ethical and moral levels of discourse in Christian ethics.

EUTHANASIA AS A MORAL PROBLEM

Although a primary goal of medical practice is the prolongation of life, there are occasions in which efforts to relieve suffering are given priority over efforts to prolong life. In terminal medical practice, medical decisions often must take into account the length and the quality of life that remains. When suffering cannot be relieved adequately, a dignified and peaceful death sometimes becomes the primary goal of medical care. In such cases, a patient whose life has been prolonged artificially may be allowed to die while every effort is made to keep him as comfortable as possible. In other cases, however, a patient who is not yet dying but whose condition is hopeless may be caused to die in order to prevent further useless suffering. The motives and the ends are the same in both cases: euthanasia (an easy death). The difference in means serves to distinguish passive euthanasia from active euthanasia. These forms of terminal medical care pose at least two basic questions for Christian medical ethics: Is there a moral distinction between allowing and causing a patient to die? Does the relief of suffering, as a motive and as an end, serve to justify means that indirectly or directly result in his death?

From the perspective of Roman Catholic medical ethics, there is a moral difference between allowing and causing a patient's death in some cases. This distinction is based on the fact that, although the negative natural law principle which forbids direct killing (causing death) is absolute, there are reasonable and proportionate limits to the affirmative natural law duty to preserve life and health. These limits are defined by a distinction between *ordinary* and *extraordinary* means to preserve life. Because ordinary means are always required, allowing a patient to die by failing to provide these measures is morally equivalent to causing his death. Because extraordinary means are optional in most cases, there is an important distinction between allowing a patient to die by omitting these measures and causing his death.

There is also a moral difference between *direct* and *indirect* killing in Catholic medical ethics. The primary factor in this distinction is the intention of the action or the omission that results in death. The practice of euthanasia constitutes direct killing, because death is intended as a means to an end, i.e., the release from suffering. Efforts to relieve suffering that unintentionally cause or hasten death constitute indirect killing. In such cases, the principle of double effect determines the moral limits of the obligation to preserve life.

Paul Ramsey insists that a distinction between allowing and causing a patient to die is required by the duty to "care for the dying." Although he acknowledges that omission and commission may sometimes be morally equivalent, he underscores the possibility that they may not be the same in every case and considers the relevance of this possibility for medical practice. On the basis of the distinction between ordinary, or "mandatory," and extraordinary, or "elective," means, Ramsey defines the moral limits of the duty to "save life" and makes room for "*only* caring for the dying." He points out that omission of elective measures is "only incidentally a 'not doing,' in order positively to care, to comfort, to be humanly present with the dying." [5]

From an entirely different conception of the basis of Christian medical ethics, Karl Barth initially denies the validity of a moral distinction between allowing and causing death to occur. He insists that the same truth which applies to active killing in terminal cases also applies to the passive failure to prolong life. Nevertheless, Barth recognizes that the artificial prolongation of life can become a forbidden torturing of it. He therefore acknowledges the possibility of an exceptional case in this special sphere. This exception would provide a basis for a distinction between allowing and causing a patient to die. Barth warns, however, that we must wait for further developments in order to get a clear picture.

In contrast with Barth, Dietrich Bonhoeffer insists that there is a fundamental moral difference between permitting a patient to die and deliberately ending his life. Underlying this distinction is his conception of life as an end in itself and as a means to an end. On the one hand, Bonhoeffer points out that the status of life as an end in itself is reflected in the rights with which it is endowed within the framework of the natural life. He deals with the question of active euthanasia in the context of his examination of the first of these natural rights, the preservation of life of the body from arbitrary killing. On the other hand, Bonhoeffer claims that the fact that life is a means to an end is expressed in the duties that are imposed on it. His brief discussion of the question of passive euthanasia suggests that this fact may also be expressed by the absence of a duty. Because life and its preservation are not solely ends in themselves, there is no absolute obligation to prolong life by artificial means.

Joseph Fletcher distinguishes between allowing and causing patients to die, but he regards this as a practical rather than as a moral distinction. It is solely for the sake of "practical conclusions" that he differentiates between *indirect* euthanasia, or "antidysthanasia," and *direct* euthanasia, or "euthanasia in its simple, unsophisticated, and ethically candid form." [6] That is, he makes this distinction simply because he recognizes that it may be easier to gain acceptance for indirect euthanasia as a first step in securing legal approval for direct euthanasia. The terms "indirect" and "direct" are borrowed from the natural law tradition in Christian ethics, but Fletcher uses them merely to distinguish procedures which cause death indirectly from those which cause death directly. Furthermore, he interprets the differences of opinion in religious circles concerning the morality of euthanasia as disagreements concerning "only the 'operational' or practical question—who does what under which circumstances?" [7]

In order to resolve the moral problems that arise in the context of terminal medical care, it is important to understand the procedural differences between allowing and causing patients to die. It is also important to recognize the difference between this operational distinction and a moral evaluation of allowing and causing a patient's death. For the purpose of analysis, a procedural distinction can be made between allowing an easy death, or *passive* euthanasia, and causing an easy death, or *active* euthanasia. On this basis, the morality of each can be examined from the perspectives of Roman Catholic and Protestant theological ethics.

THE MORALITY OF PASSIVE EUTHANASIA

The Catholic Church does not make a distinction between passive and active euthanasia. From this perspective, deliberately allowing a terminal patient to die solely for the purpose of relieving his suffering is morally equivalent to direct killing and thus constitutes a grave moral evil. Furthermore, the failure to provide ordinary means to preserve life, for whatever reason, is usually regarded as direct killing. There is a decisive difference, however, between killing a patient and ceasing to make extraordinary efforts to keep him alive. This distinction is based on the fact that natural law requires only that ordinary measures be used to prolong life. In order to understand the relevance of this distinction to the problem of suffering in terminal medical care, it is necessary to examine the way in which "ordinary" means and "extraordinary" means are interpreted in Catholic medical ethics.

Gerald Kelly points out that doctors and theologians tend to attach different meanings to these terms. On the one hand, physicians regard "ordinary" measures as "standard, recognized, orthodox, or established medicines or procedures of that period, at that level of medical practice, and within the limits of availability." [8] They consider "extraordinary" measures as procedures that are "fanciful, bizarre, experimental, incompletely established, unorthodox, or not recognized." [9] On the other hand, theologians interpret "ordinary" measures to include "all medicines, treatments, and operations which offer a reasonable hope of benefit for the patient and which can be obtained and used without excessive expense, pain, or other inconvenience." [10] They identify as "extraordinary" measures "all medicines, treatments, and operations which cannot be obtained or used without excessive expense, pain, or other inconvenience, or if used would not offer a reasonable hope of benefit." [11] According to Kelly, "convenience" and "utility" are the basic criteria underlying these standards for evaluating all artificial life-sustainers. He insists that they are extraordinary if either of these conditions is lacking.

There is general agreement among prominent Catholic moral theologians concerning the principles for distinguishing between ordinary and extraordinary measures. Nevertheless, there are important differences in their application of these principles. Some theologians make this distinction only with regard to artificial measures to prolong life. Edwin F. Healy, Charles J. McFadden, and Thomas J. O'Donnell, for example, consider natural measures, such as normal food, drink, and rest, as ordinary means which are required in every case. Artificial measures, including drugs, oxygen, and surgical operation, are judged to be either ordinary or extraordinary in relation to the circumstances of each case.[12]

Other theologians, however, apply the criteria for distinguishing between ordinary and extraordinary measures to both natural and artificial means to prolong life. Kelly uses the term "ordinary" to describe natural means and artificial means that are usually employed as temporary remedies. By judging whether ordinary measures are morally required with reference to their "convenience" and "utility," he establishes a basis, at least in principle, for omitting natural as well as artificial means. Joseph V. Sullivan distinguishes between mandatory and optional means to prolong life on the basis of the principle that a natural means which is ordinary *per se* may be extraordinary *per accidens* and an artificial means may be ordinary or extraordinary relative to the condition of the patient.

Catholic theologians differ not only in their analyses of natural means to preserve life but also in their evaluations of artificial means. This is reflected, for example, in conflicting interpretations of intravenous feeding as in cases such as the following, which is described by Sullivan:

> A cancer patient is in extreme pain and his system has
> gradually established what physicians call "toleration" of any

drug, so that even increased doses give only brief respite from the ever-recurring pain. The attending physician knows that the person is slowly dying, but because of a good heart, it is possible that his agony will continue for several weeks. The physician then remembers that there is one thing he can do to end the suffering. He can cut off intravenous feeding and the patient will surely die. He does this and before the next day the patient is dead.[13]

In response to a similar case, Joseph P. Donovan argues that intravenous feeding must be considered an ordinary means of preserving life. He claims that this treatment is neither physically nor morally impossible and thus concludes that stopping it would be equivalent to mercy killing. Kelly also interprets intravenous feeding as an ordinary measure but suggests that there is no sound reason to require that a patient submit to it when it is "relatively useless." Sullivan acknowledges that intravenous feeding is an ordinary procedure in most cases. He concludes, however, that "since this cancer patient is beyond all hope of recovery and suffering extreme pain, intravenous feeding should be considered an extraordinary means of prolonging life." On this basis he insists that the physician is justified in stopping such treatment when he is certain that the patient is spiritually prepared to die. McFadden agrees with this evaluation of intravenous feeding. He indicates that theoretically it would seem morally permissible to discontinue its use in this case. Nevertheless, both he and Kelly oppose this as a practice. They claim that this might be misunderstood and interpreted as a "Catholic euthanasia." They also warn that this practice would be extended to other types of cases.

Although Bernard Häring recognizes this danger, he cautions that "we have to be most careful not to rush in with a negative judgment."[14] From Häring's perspective, the direct intention for withdrawing medical treatment is more important than the question of whether the measure is ordinary or extraordinary. Thus in order to come to terms with the morality of what he calls "negative" euthanasia, he makes two important distinctions. In the first place, he points out that it is one thing to suppress undesirable pain and anxiety, even if the patient's life is thereby shortened, and it is another thing deliberately to hasten death. In the second place, he argues that stopping treatments that really prolong life is different from stopping treatments that only prolong the process of dying. In each of these distinctions, the crucial factor is the intention with which an omission or an action is undertaken. Häring does not condone the deliberate taking of life by direct or indirect means. He does, however, permit premeditated omissions of treatment in order to prevent suffering which is contrary to the idea of dying with dignity and peace. Furthermore, it is only when the decision is based on such criteria as freedom, responsibility, loving care, and human dignity that negative or passive euthanasia is acceptable. If it is unduly enlarged or if strictly utilitarian considerations enter in, Häring insists that this form of euthanasia must be formally rejected.

In spite of differences of opinion among Catholic theologians concerning the requirements of terminal medical care, they agree that there is no absolute obligation to preserve life by every available means in every case. They are also sensitive to a broad range of humane considerations in providing moral guidelines for terminal decisions. Although most theologians do not accept mercy or sympathy as a rationale for deliberately allowing a suffering patient to die, they take his suffering into account in determining whether efforts to prolong his life are extraordinary. The omission or cessation of such measures, which are judged to be morally optional, constitutes passive euthanasia. Even though most Catholic moralists refrain from using this term, they sanction omissions that allow patients to die.

Paul Ramsey interprets this practice as a means of caring for the dying. Because he defines "euthanasia" as direct killing, he considers this term to be inappropriate to describe ceasing to prolong life. He distinguishes between acts of euthanasia and "only caring for the dying" on the basis of a moral distinction between commission and omission. Ramsey insists that an omission only allows the patient to die from causes against which it is no longer reasonable or merciful to fight by means of medical interventions. In order to emphasize the positive quality of caring for the dying in this way, he describes it as "ceasing to do something that was once begun in order to do something that is better because now more fitting." [15]

Ramsey recognizes the wisdom and value of past moral reflection for contemporary medical practice involving fatally ill and dying patients. He points out that within traditional medical ethics and natural law moral philosophy the *generic* duty to "save life" is applied with reference to *moral-species* terms distinguishing between ordinary and extraordinary measures. He acknowledges that these are "empty" concepts but claims that this relativity in their meaning constitutes a chief virtue of this distinction. In order to explain what is morally required in caring for the dying, Ramsey distinguishes the way in which moralists interpret and use these terms from the way in which physicians understand and apply them. Furthermore, he suggests specific "*reforming* definitions," or "creative lines of development" of these moral concepts for terminal medical decisions.

In the first place, Ramsey observes that doctors usually interpret the terms "ordinary" and "extraordinary" relative to "customary" and "unusual" medical practices. He claims that they tend to require the use of every established or customary procedure in order to save life. This is said to be due not only to the threat of malpractice suits, which might be brought against them if they depart too far from accepted standards of medical practice. It is also attributed to the fact that their consciences are formed in these terms. Thus, physicians are able to justify omitting unusual or "heroic" efforts much more readily than they can justify omitting or stopping customary measures. Consequently, the medical imperative changes in accordance with advances in the practice of medicine, as unusual or "extraordinary" procedures become customary or "ordinary."

Ramsey insists that the medical imperative ought to change according to the changes or "advances" of the patient's condition as well as in relation to changing standards of medical practice. He points out that moralists use the terms "ordinary" and "extraordinary" in relation to a patient's particular condition rather than in connection with medical practices for patients in general. Furthermore, he indicates how far Roman Catholic moral theologians are willing to go in qualifying the imperative to use even the so-called ordinary means of preserving life. In order to complete an ethics of caring for the dying, Ramsey proposes two additional qualifications of this traditional moral distinction, between "mandatory" and "elective" efforts to save life. These reforming or liberalizing definitions of the obligation to care for the dying are stated in the following terms: "(1) . . . there is no duty to use *useless* means, however natural or ordinary or customary in practice and (2) . . . the description of human acts of caring for the dying (or caring for the not yet dying) terminates in *the man* who is the patient of these ministrations and not in the disease or diseases he has." [16]

In the second place, Ramsey claims that physicians seem to find it more difficult to justify stopping extraordinary life-sustaining measures than to justify not starting them. He notes that moralists sanction omitting and interrupting such procedures on the basis of the same moral warrants.

From Ramsey's perspective, there should be no greater reluctance on the part of the doctor to conclude that the continuation of efforts to prolong life is no longer indicated than to decide that the efforts should not be instituted. He interprets the doctor-patient relationship as a covenant that the patient enters for complete care and not for continuing useless efforts to cure. Furthermore, he points out that in order to provide appropriate care the doctor must decide when medical procedures offer "no reasonable hope" and determine the onset of an irreversible "process of dying." According to Ramsey, the moral imperative and the medical imperative are the same at this point. Because there is no obligation to employ useless remedies, he insists that either of these conditions constitutes a sufficient and morally obliging warrant for terminating the use of medical means to sustain life.

In the third place, Ramsey suggests that physicians and moralists tend to disagree concerning the relevance of nonmedical factors in distinguishing between ordinary and extraordinary efforts to save life. He acknowledges that, *as men* who are doctors, physicians may take a number of human (nonmedical) considerations into account in decisions having to do with terminal medical care. Nevertheless, he contends that these would not be strictly medical decisions and that they would not correspond with their usual interpretation of the distinction between ordinary and extraordinary means. According to Ramsey, moral theologians almost always understand this distinction to refer to nonmedical factors such as the inconvenience, the expense, the pain, and the benefit of efforts to prolong life. He points out that they intend to counsel first the patient and his family, and then the physician, that in distinguishing between imperative and elective measures it is appropriate to make a "balancing judgment" involving decisive reference to morally relevant human factors in each case.

Ramsey underscores the fact that for terminal medical care the moral imperative is more comprehensive than the medical imperative. He insists that not only morally relevant medical features of practices and patients but also nonmedical features must be taken into account in evaluating measures for prolonging life and in determining the proper course to follow for each patient. On the one hand, he maintains that human, familial, and neighborly values may require that otherwise imperative life-sustaining procedures be omitted or interrupted. Ramsey points out that these factors have always kept the saving of life from becoming an absolute and inflexible norm in Christian medical ethics. On the other hand, he claims that there are considerations, such as a patient's importance to the common good and his fiduciary relations with his fellowmen and with God, which may require the use of measures to prolong life which are elective in most cases. Ramsey therefore argues that a doctor should "lean against" his understanding of the medical imperative in order to make room for the primacy of human moral judgments on the part of his patients, their relatives, and their spiritual counselors.

Karl Barth, however, does not regard these factors as valid criteria for terminal medical decisions. He insists that human life belongs solely to God and that it can be taken only in response to a clear and specific command of God. Barth charges that those who sponsor euthanasia fail to take into account this central insight of Christian ethics. He acknowledges that there are tempting arguments in favor of putting an end to a patient's suffering by mercifully not applying means for the artificial prolongation of his life. Nevertheless, he claims that these arguments contain too much sophistry for those who are directed by the command of God to accept.

According to Barth, the command to respect and to protect human life requires its preservation. He therefore argues that no one may "give up" the life of a sick person either by encompassing his death or by letting his life ebb away. In response to arguments for euthanasia on the basis of the "humanitarianism of underlying motive," he contends that subjectively well-meaning motives do not change wrong into right. Furthermore, Barth warns that we can never be certain that we are really helping a patient by assisting him to die. In the last analysis, he concludes that euthanasia cannot possibly be justified before the command of God, and that it cannot therefore be undertaken and executed in obedience to it.

Barth strongly insists that this conclusion applies to the passive failure to provide stimulants that artifically prolong life. From his perspective, deliberately allowing a patient to die is morally equivalent to intentionally taking his life. It is important to note, however, that Barth recognizes the possibility that efforts to keep a patient alive might amount to human arrogance in the opposite direction. His commitment to the command of God to respect and to protect life not only leads him to affirm the medical imperative to preserve life but it also leads him to question "whether the fulfillment of the medical duty does not threaten to become fanaticism, reason folly, and the required assisting of human life a forbidden torturing of it." [17] Because of the respect that may be claimed by dying life as such, Barth suggests that an exceptional case is at least conceivable in which a doctor would have to refrain from prolonging life no less than from terminating it. Although he cautions that further insight is required in this special sphere, he indicates that such an exception might be possible, since it would not be arbitrary euthanasia to allow a patient to die in this case.

Dietrich Bonhoeffer observes that there are situations in which doctors do not employ every possible means in order to prolong life. Like Barth, he does not regard these as instances of arbitrary killing. Unlike Barth, however, he does not interpret such cases as occasions of exceptional obedience to the command of God to respect human life. According to Bonhoeffer, the life of the body possesses an "innate" right to its own preservation. He claims that this first right of natural life secures innocent life from deliberate destruction. Nevertheless, he does not suggest that it requires that every conceivable effort be made to postpone death.

Bonhoeffer insists that there is a basic difference between killing and allowing to die. On the one hand, he interprets euthanasia as the deliberate destruction of innocent life. On the basis of the natural right to bodily life he concludes that (active) euthanasia is never permitted. On the other hand, Bonhoeffer does not consider the failure to prolong life artificially as intentional killing. He points out, for example, that to refrain from sending a tubercular mental defective to a sanatorium is not equivalent to deliberately ending his life. Because of this distinction, Bonhoeffer does not use the term "euthanasia" to describe actions or omissions that permit suffering patients to die. Furthermore, his conclusion with regard to the morality of (active) euthanasia does not apply to cases in which doctors allow patients to die in order to end their suffering.

In contrast with moral theologians who recognize a moral difference between *allowing* to die and *causing* to die, Joseph Fletcher insists that this is a "very cloudy distinction." He points out that a decision to do nothing to prolong a patient's life is as morally deliberate as a decision to terminate his life. Furthermore, he argues that the intention is the same in either case. Fletcher concludes that the "principle of mercy death" is generally accepted and that there are differences of opinion only with regard to practical questions concerning its application. Because of resistance to active euthanasia, however, he initially suggests that it is practical to attempt first to secure legal approval for passive euthanasia.

Because the term "euthanasia" is "psychologically difficult," Fletcher refers to passive euthanasia as "dysthanasia." In the article in which he introduces this term, he defines it as "the *indirect* ending of a hard or bad death," and predicts that it will become as current as the word "euthanasia." In a subsequent revision of this essay in his *Moral Responsibility*, Fletcher takes into account the literal meaning of "dysthanasia" and replaces it with the term "antidysthanasia." He indicates that this can take any one of three forms: "(1) administering a death-dealing pain killer, (2) stopping treatment altogether, simply not doing anything to prolong a patient's dying, and (3) withholding treatment altogether, simply not doing anything first or last to keep the patient alive." [18] With regard to the problem of deciding who should make the decision for or against passive euthanasia, Fletcher claims that most terminal patients are incompetent when this question arises. He therefore interprets antidysthanasia as "a course of action or inaction whereby the patient's death is indirectly achieved, deliberately and voluntarily by the patient's attendants, whether the patient has ever expressed a wish for it or not." [19] He notes parenthetically, however, that the case would be completely different if the patient has ever expressed opposition to it.

Since the publication of *Moral Responsibility*, Fletcher has suggested a somewhat different evaluation of the morality of passive euthanasia. In response to an article advocating active euthanasia, he reintroduces the term "dysthanasia" to describe passive euthanasia. In this context, however, he intends to characterize it as a "bad death, ugly and prolonged, rather than a good death, merciful and quick." [20] He insists that a policy that permits only indirect euthanasia is based on a morality that is vitalistic and idolatrous. This underscores Fletcher's suggestion that approval for passive euthanasia is only a temporary and intermediate position. More recently, he has apparently concluded that this transitional step is no longer necessary. His position now is that the question of "negative" euthanasia is settled ethically and that further arguments are "merely flogging a dead horse." [21]

THE MORALITY OF ACTIVE EUTHANASIA

Roman Catholic moral theologians distinguish between causing death *intentionally* and causing death *unintentionally* on the basis of a moral distinction between direct and indirect killing. It is important to note, however, that they tend to use the term "euthanasia" only with reference to direct or deliberate killing in order to end suffering. Depending upon who makes the decision in each case, deliberately causing an easy death (active euthanasia) is usually interpreted as suicide, murder, or a combination of both. The position of most Catholic theologians with regard to the morality of these forms of (active) euthanasia is stated concisely in "Directive 21" of the *Ethical and Religious Directives for Catholic Hospitals:* "Euthanasia ('mercy killing') in all its forms is forbidden." [22] There are two basic theological premises underlying this conclusion: the inviolability of human life and the value of suffering.

In the first place, the practice of euthanasia is condemned on the basis of revelation (divine positive law) and reason (natural law). Gerald Kelly insists that euthanasia is contrary to the revealed law of God. He points out that "in the Holy Scriptures we have these clear statements: 'The innocent and just man thou shalt not put to death.' (Exodus 23:7) and 'The innocent and just thou shalt not kill.' (Daniel

13:53 [i.e., Susanna, v. 53])." [23] Joseph V. Sullivan argues that according to natural law, God has sovereign dominion over human life and man has no right to destroy his life unless he is commanded or permitted to do so by God. Furthermore, Sullivan cites Thomas Aquinas' argument against suicide on the basis of man's natural inclination, or appetite, to continue and to perfect his being. He concludes that "from this universal desire to live we have a strong argument against direct killing of the innocent, and hence against all forms of euthanasia." [24]

In the second place, the practice of euthanasia is rejected as a denial of the spiritual significance of suffering. Norman St. John-Stevas explains that although Catholics regard suffering as an evil in the natural order, they recognize that it is not an absolute evil and that it has redeeming features. Sullivan's argument against euthanasia is based on an even more affirmative evaluation of suffering. He insists that a measure of suffering is necessary for man's perfection and is given by God in accordance with each man's needs. Furthermore, he declares that it is the mark of a good and holy God that He allows so many to suffer on earth in order to atone for imperfections and sin. Sullivan concludes that "suffering is almost the greatest gift of God's love." [25] Kelly also opposes euthanasia on the basis of this conception of the value of suffering. He argues that those who favor its practice ignore the fact "that no one suffers save through the will of God; that through suffering a man can beautify his character, atone for his sins, take a special part in the sublime work of Redemption, and win for himself an eternity of Glory." [26]

In spite of this affirmation of the value of suffering, the importance of providing the necessary relief is emphasized in Roman Catholic medical ethics. In an address to the Italian Society for the Science of Anaesthetics in February, 1957, Pope Pius XII insisted that one is never obligated to endure suffering for its own sake. In response to questions concerning the use of analgesic treatments in terminal cases, the pope found that "direct euthanasia" is always unlawful. Nevertheless, he concluded that the use of drugs that tend to shorten lives is lawful in order to relieve suffering if such drugs have two distinct effects—the relief of suffering and the shortening of life—and if there is no causal link between these effects. As Bernard Häring points out, there is no reluctance in the Catholic tradition to approve of treatment with the direct purpose of relieving pain and anxiety, even if these hasten death. Positive euthanasia, i.e., the direct hastening of death to relieve suffering, is said to be an altogether different question, and Häring strongly opposes this practice.[27]

The principal moral distinctions in traditional Catholic discussions of euthanasia differentiate between omission and commission and between direct and indirect killing. Although these are important moral distinctions, liberal Catholic moralists question whether they are applicable in every case and whether there are proportionate reasons to allow or to cause a patient to die. Daniel C. Maguire underscores the importance of the new emphasis on proportionality as opening the way to a revolution in Catholic ethics on such questions as euthanasia. He acknowledges, however, that this change leads to greater ambiguity and to difficult moral decisions. In spite of serious objections, he concludes that the morality of mercy killing is at least probable in certain circumstances, due to intrinsic reasons and the inadequacy of opposing views.[28]

In cases in which "the ending of life is the best that life offers," [29] is there a moral difference between an omission and a commission that results in death? Maguire responds to this question with reference to a case that occurred in 1971 at Johns Hopkins University Hospital when parents refused life-saving surgery for a mongoloid baby. He argues that while the death of this child may have been merciful, the dying was not. Maguire further suggests that the omission might have been immoral without an act to shorten the final fifteen days of torture. In this case, he seems to find it harder to justify omission than commission.[30]

Charles E. Curran answers the question of the moral difference between omission and commission by distinguishing between persons who are living and persons who are dying. For the living, this is considered to be an important distinction, because man does not have full dominion over his life. Thus he cannot interfere to take his life directly. For the dying, however, Curran does not find a significant difference between acts of omission and acts of commission, because man has dominion over his bodily processes, including the process of dying. When a patient is dying, man's positive intervention is said to be in keeping with the process rather than an arrogant usurping of the role of God. Curran recognizes the practical problems of defining and providing criteria for determining the dying process and the danger that justifying any direct interference will lead to a broader endorsement of mercy killing. Nevertheless, he proposes a tentative case for active euthanasia at the same point in which treatments can be discontinued because they are useless.[31]

Paul Ramsey recognizes that the needs and claims of suffering patients who are dying are radically different from those patients who are not yet dying. Nevertheless, he argues that "a religious outlook that goes with grace among the dying can never be compatible with euthanasiac acts or sentiments." [32] According to Ramsey, appropriate "treatment" for the dying is care and comfort. Any effort to hasten a dying patient beyond the reach of love and care is viewed as a defection from their faithfulness-claims. Nevertheless, Ramsey acknowledges that death-hastening painkillers may be given in order to relieve suffering. He

interprets this as an expression of care for the dying which is
analogous to a drink of cool water for his comfort. The
justification for this relief of suffering, which also hastens
death, is that it is a "direct voluntary" action, and the
administration of the drug is only an "indirect voluntary"
way.

The basic norm underlying Ramsey's position with regard
to the morality of active euthanasia is the "*categorical*
imperative: never abandon care!" In order to probe the
meaning of this requirement for cases in which patients are
no longer capable of being given and receiving care and
comfort, he poses the question: "Is it morally permissible
directly to terminate life that is beyond all human caring?" [33] Ramsey suggests that there are at least two
situations in which this question might be applicable. In the
first place, it might be relevant to cases involving patients in
deep and irreversible coma whose lives are maintained for
many years. In the second place, it might apply to cases in
which patients are undergoing deep and prolonged pain
that cannot be relieved. Ramsey points out that, if his
analysis is correct, it is a matter of complete indifference to
these patients whether death is allowed to come directly or
indirectly. He concludes that there is no moral difference
between omission and commission in such cases because the
obligation to care for the dying, which is the rationale for
this distinction, can no longer be fulfilled.

On the basis of this conclusion, Ramsey proposes these
qualifications or "exceptions" to the duty always to care for
the dying:

> 1. Never abandon care of the dying except when they are
> irretrievably inaccessible to human care, never hasten the
> dying process except when it is *entirely indifferent* to the
> patient whether his dying is accomplished by an intravenous
> bubble of air or by the withdrawal of useless ordinary natural
> remedies, such as nourishment.

2. Always keep officious treatments away from the dying in order to draw close to them in companying with them and caring for them, never, therefore, take positive action to usher them out of our presence or to hasten their departure from the human community, unless there is a kind of prolonged dying in which it is medically impossible to keep severe pain at bay.[34]

Ramsey is especially concerned not to compromise the moral duty to care for the dying. He believes that, rather than weakening this rule, these qualifications extend the meaning of this duty in order to comprehend problematic cases. He warns, however, that it does not at once follow that the *rules of practice* governing medical care should include these exceptions. Nevertheless, he concludes that within their strict limitations, these qualifications of the categorical imperative to care for the dying can be admitted as practice rules without weakening medicine's impulse to save life.

Since his discussion of the requirements of care for the dying in *The Patient as Person*, Ramsey has had second thoughts concerning the acceptance of death. The principal source of his qualms is the sudden popularity of this position. Specifically, he objects to superficial campaigns for "death with dignity" which fail to understand the dignity of human life. As a confessed controversialist in ethics, Ramsey rejects such appeals, arguing instead the ultimate indignity of death. He claims, for example, that "there is an additional insult besides death itself heaped upon the dying by our ordinary talk about 'death with dignity.' " [35] With this in mind, one would be hesitant to embrace Ramsey's exceptions to the imperative to care for the dying as the basis for an appeal for active euthanasia. It is important to note, however, that in spite of his emphasis on the indignity of death Ramsey does not reinterpret this imperative to require that life be prolonged and death avoided as long as possible. Instead, he argues that care for the dying requires that our conception of "dying with dignity" encompass the final indignity of death.

In contrast with Ramsey, Karl Barth argues that it is "casuistical frivolity" to presume to determine an exceptional case apart from an unequivocal command of God. Because he recognizes that human life has no absolute greatness or ultimate value, Barth acknowledges the possibility of an exception to the obligation to preserve and to defend it. He claims that "God as the Lord of life may further its protection even in the strange form of its conclusion and termination rather than its preservation and advancement." [36] Paul Ramsey interprets this as "love's 'casuistry' . . . seeking to overleap principles." [37] Barth, however, points out that the possibility of this exception is always the particular possibility of God himself. He warns that it can be conceived of and accepted "only as *ultima ratio*, only as highly exceptional, and therefore only with the greatest reserve on the exhaustion of all other possibilities." [38]

In his analysis of the command of God in the sphere of creation, Barth insists that the Biblical command "Thou shalt not kill" requires the affirmation and protection of human life. He explains that, when this command is understood in its final New Testament form, we cannot exclude the possibility of an exceptional case and we cannot assert too emphatically that any case is exceptional. Nevertheless, he maintains that only God can take life and that man should help only in response to a clear and specific command of God. Because he finds that this form of deliberate killing can never seem to be really commanded in any emergency, Barth concludes that euthanasia cannot be anything but murder.

Dietrich Bonhoeffer evaluates the morality of active euthanasia in relation to the natural right to preserve one's bodily life. He interprets this right as the foundation of the entire framework of the rights and duties of natural life, which is preserved by God after the Fall. It is important to note that Bonhoeffer regards the life of the body both as an end in itself and as a means to an end. On the one hand, he points out that it carries within itself the right to its own preservation. This first right of natural life consists in the safeguarding of bodily life from arbitrary killing. On the other hand, he claims that the life of the body is not only a gift that is to be preserved but also a sacrifice that is to be offered. The right or duty to sacrifice one's body, however, presupposes the underlying right to conserve one's bodily life.

Bonhoeffer affirms the principle that "all deliberate killing of innocent life is arbitrary." [39] Nevertheless, he examines the possibility that active euthanasia might constitute an exception to this principle. He suggests that there are two motives behind the arguments for euthanasia: consideration for the sick and consideration for the healthy. Before evaluating these arguments, Bonhoeffer asserts (as a matter of principle) that taking another's life can be justified only on the basis of an unconditional necessity. He therefore insists that any argument in favor of euthanasia must be decisive in itself. Furthermore, he warns that efforts to justify the practice of euthanasia by appealing to a number of essentially different arguments indirectly admits that there is no single, absolutely cogent justification of it.

According to Bonhoeffer, arguments for euthanasia out of regard for the incurably sick must presuppose their assent or wish to die. He points out that it can hardly be said that the patient is being considered when this desire is not expressed or when there is an unmistakable demand to remain alive. He suggests that the same is true in cases involving mentally defective patients whose assent or desire cannot be explicitly uttered and in cases involving acutely depressed patients who also are not their own masters. With regard to the appeal for euthanasia on behalf of incurable patients who are in full possession of their senses and request to die, Bonhoeffer argues that this demand is not valid so long as the patient's life makes its own demand. He insists that the doctor has an obligation to the actual life of the patient as well as to his will. In the last analysis, he concludes that consideration for the patient is not an adequate basis for the necessity of destroying human life.

Arguments for euthanasia out of concern for the healthy are said to presuppose that the value of life consists solely in its usefulness to society. Bonhoeffer, however, claims that life possesses an inherent value which has nothing to do with its social worth. From his perspective, there is no life that is not worth living, because life itself is valued by God. He warns that to regard either utility or health as the highest value would ultimately destroy everyone's right to life. For these reasons, Bonhoeffer argues that deliberate killing of the innocent sick cannot be justified on the basis of consideration for the healthy. Nevertheless, he suggests that judgment should at least be suspended in cases in which incurable patients take their own lives for the sake of their families. Although Bonhoeffer underscores the general principle that one should not commit suicide, he insists that this principle cannot be made absolute to the exclusion of the right to sacrifice one's life.

Joseph Fletcher regards the law of love as the only absolute norm of Christian ethics. He claims that the validity of all moral principles is contingent upon the requirements of love in each situation. Fletcher therefore rejects the principles of medical ethics which categorically forbid active euthanasia. He insists that they are products of a vitalism which destroys personal integrity and a fatalism which denies human freedom. Underlying his evaluation of these principles and his position with regard to the morality of active euthanasia is a personalistic view of the meaning and value of life.

According to Fletcher, human "life" involves more than mere vital existence. He underscores the importance of such personal qualities as freedom, knowledge, self-possession and control, and responsibility. Furthermore, he claims that the preservation of these values can justify the loss of life. In opposition to the determinism which he finds in the moral and legal norms governing the practice of medicine, Fletcher insists that man, as a spiritual being, has a right to exercise intelligent control over his physical nature. On this basis, he endorses both "indirect" and "direct" euthanasia and argues that death control is a matter of human dignity.

Fletcher points out that there are three different schools of thought in support of the practice of euthanasia. One favors voluntary euthanasia for patients with incurable and fatal physical suffering. Another recommends involuntary euthanasia for monstrosities at birth and for mental defectives. Still another approves of involuntary euthanasia for all who are a burden on the community. Fletcher accepts the first two of these schools of thought. He interprets the first as a personalistic ethical position and the second as a partly personalistic and partly eugenic position. He describes the third position as purely eugenic and insists that its acceptance is not required by the approval of either or both of the other points of view.

From Fletcher's perspective, there is no real moral difference between self-administered euthanasia and medically administered euthanasia when it is done at a patient's request. Given his acceptance of suicide as a form of voluntary euthanasia which serves to protect and fulfill human dignity, his justification for voluntary euthanasia follows on the basis of the "time honored rule that what one may lawfully do another may help him to do." [40] Fletcher's argument for involuntary euthanasia is necessarily based on entirely different presuppositions. His primary justification for terminating the lives of radically deformed infants and severe retardates is that they are not human beings. Fletcher claims, for example, that there is no cause for guilt or remorse over lethally "putting away" a Down's syndrome baby, because "a Down's is not a person." [41] This rationale for taking life, however, has nothing to do with the question of euthanasia. In the last analysis, the term "euthanasia" is appropriate only when a patient takes his own life or when his life is taken in his behalf in order to relieve or to prevent his suffering.

THE ETHICS OF RESPONSE

Protestant and Catholic theologians are increasingly aware of the moral dilemmas that arise in the context of terminal medical care. They recognize the responsibility of Christian ethics in relation to these problems. Furthermore, they share a common faith in God as the basis for interpreting ethical principles and ordering moral norms for medical decisions. Nevertheless, much of the controversy in the debate over euthanasia stems from fundamentally different conceptions of the relationship between faith commitments, ethical principles, and moral standards for the practice of medicine.

A typology delineated by H. Richard Niebuhr serves to call attention to some of the underlying, conceptual differences in the conflicting arguments concerning euthanasia in theological ethics. [42] According to Niebuhr, there are three basic images of man as a moral agent that are implicit both in theoretical ethics and in practical decisions. The first image is that of "man-the-maker." This symbol of man as an artist or a craftsman, who constructs things according to an idea and for the sake of an end, is characteristic of teleological ethics, which seeks to direct life toward the *good*. The second image is that of "man-the-citizen." The symbol of the citizen living under laws is characteristic of deontological ethics, which attempts to order life in accordance with the *right*. The third image is that of "man-the-answerer." The symbol of man engaged in dialogue is characteristic of "response ethics," which seeks to orient life in relation to what is *fitting*.

Niebuhr's evaluation of teleological and deontological ethics is especially interesting insofar as the question of euthanasia is concerned. Purposive ethics, such as situational ethics, seeks to resolve this question with reference to fundamental goals or ideals. Ethical principles and moral norms serve as guidelines to these ends. Part of the meaning of suffering, as Niebuhr points out, is that it "cuts athwart our purposive movements." [43] An ethics of duty, such as natural law ethics or Barth's ethics, attempts to resolve the question of euthanasia in relation to basic laws or duties. Ethical principles and moral rules define the requirements of these ultimate norms. Suffering, however, reveals the presence of that which is not under man's control and which operates under another law. Thus, Niebuhr concludes that neither teleological ethics nor deontological ethics provides an adequate basis for an ethics of suffering.

The ethics of responsibility begins with responses rather than with purposes or laws. It seeks to understand the self, not as it is in itself, but as it is in response relationships. Because a response ethics is concerned with the fitting response, it asks first the question: "What is going on?" According to Niebuhr, the idea or pattern of responsibility makes suffering intelligible in a way in which the pattern of teleology and deontology cannot. It deals with the problem of human suffering in terms of man's response as a moral agent. From this point of view, euthanasia can be evaluated as a response to suffering.

In order to understand what is required of man from a theological perspective, it is important to begin with the way in which God is related to man and man is responsible to God. In the Christian tradition, God is understood in Trinitarian terms as Father, Son, and Holy Spirit. These symbols represent God as he is in himself. The way in which he is understood in relation to man is expressed in additional symbols for God such as Creator, Judge, and Redeemer. Although each of these symbols is open to a broad range of interpretations, there are basic conclusions that can be drawn with regard to what is required of man in response to God.

The ultimate basis of Christian faith is the revelation of God's love in Christ. It is from this perspective that all the symbols that represent God in relation to man are interpreted. As Creator, God brings into being and sustains the universe. The life of Christ reveals the nature of God as a personal and loving Father. Consequently, the entire universe is understood as an expression of his love. As Judge, God governs and protects the world that he creates. The death of Christ discloses not only the sin of man but also the depth of God's love. Thus, the judgment of God is recognized as the stern discipline of his love. As Redeemer, God overcomes the destructive power of sin and death. The resurrection of Christ demonstrates the mercy and forgiveness of God's redemptive love. In this light, the grace of God is perceived reconciling man with God, with his neighbor, and with himself.

Corresponding with the love of God, Christian ethics is an ethics of responsive love. In response to God as Creator, responsible love values the entire universe as it is created and sustained by God. It therefore cares for everything that exists in proper relation to the ultimate Source of being and value. Love that corresponds with the love of God accords man the highest priority in the order of nature. It responds to the needs and desires of all men as fellow creatures and children of God. Therefore, a medical ethics that is based on theocentric love is patient-oriented. It requires that each patient be cared for as a person rather than treated as a client or as a case.

Love that is responsible to God as Judge is responsive to his governing action in the world. It recognizes the sovereignty of God in the structures of the natural order and in the limitations and the potentialities of human existence. In medical care, responsible love engages in the ordering work of God in the context of specific cases. It discerns the will and the power of God in the processes that give life and health and in those that cause suffering and death. Love that corresponds with the love of God cares for the living and the dying. Nevertheless, it respects the limits that are imposed on life by God. Consequently, in making life and death decisions in terminal medical care, it does not attempt to "play God" by assuming an unlimited right either to prolong life or to take life.

The love of God as Redeemer tempers his justice with mercy and reconciles God and man. In response to his redeeming love, all our responses are transformed. Because the grace of God transcends his judgment, one is able to respond to everything that happens, including suffering and death, with confidence and hope rather than with fear and despair. Such trust is expressed and confirmed in the life, death, and resurrection of Christ. From this perspective, all interpretations of life and death are reinterpreted. As Niebuhr points out, "death no less than life appears to us as an act of mercy, not of mercy to *us* only, but in the great vicariousness of responsive and responsible existence, as mercy to those in whom, with whom, and for whom we live." [44]

This transformation leads inevitably to a reconsideration of ethical principles and moral norms having to do with medical care for the dying. If euthanasia is required in response to the needs of suffering and dying patients, responsible love must challenge and reform conventional moral and legal norms that forbid the practice. On the basis of the requirements of love in the context of terminal medical care, it must seek to create responsible guidelines for medical decisions. In so doing, it is important not only to take into account the insights of moral theologians but also join in the dialogue with medical and legal authorities who are concerned with this problem. In the following chapters, the question of euthanasia is examined in the light of scientific and technological innovations in the field of medicine and in relation to accepted professional and legal standards of medical practice.

4
MEDICAL DILEMMAS
IN TERMINAL CARE

Euthanasia is one of an entire spectrum of problems that have been created or intensified by recent advances in medical science and technology. In the first place, an unprecedented reorientation has occurred in the structure of medical practice because of the increasing differentiation within the expanding range of its competence and because of growing demands on its services. The classic doctor-patient relationship no longer provides a sufficient basis for understanding the contemporary structure and function of medical practice. Neither does it provide an adequate context within which responsible decisions can be made regarding the use of many of the procedures that are now available. Nevertheless, this traditional conception continues to prevail among the majority of its members as well as in the legal system and in society in general.

In the second place, as a result of our phenomenal technological achievements, public expectations have increased far beyond the abilities of the physician. The prevention and conquest of one disease after another has created the illusion that death, too, is vulnerable to our attack. To medical science is attributed the power to perform miracles "which can effectively pull back dying men from the edge of the grave." [1] Thus the doctor has come to personify the public's optimism and insistence that all problems can and must be solved. So long as he remains the central figure during serious illness, everyone is assured that the patient has a chance.

In the third place, while the medical profession has contributed both to the quality of life and to its quantity, the easy compatibility of these two objectives can no longer be taken for granted. When the means by which one can be attained compromises the other, decisions have to be made between these traditional coordinate values that have so long served as the moral basis of medical practice. Such choices, usually difficult, are made with great uncertainty in the absence of a clear priority of values and norms.

In the fourth place, our cultural orientation toward death, which once was based on religious beliefs interpreting its meaning, has been radically secularized in the wake of the scientific and technological revolution. The rituals and ceremonies surrounding death, which once served to assuage our grief, loss, hostility, guilt, and fear in the face of death, have become hollow and ineffective. Yet, unlike some other of our former taboos (such as sex) which we strive to confront realistically, death is increasingly avoided and disguised. Consequently, we are forced to internalize our thoughts, feelings, and fears to an unhealthy degree.

Because of these disorientations in our customary points of view, difficult medical decisions in cases of terminal illness or fatal injury are extremely problematical. The physician is under tremendous pressure to assume and maintain the central role and is regarded as the protector of human life. Between the borders of his ability to cure and the limits of his ability to alleviate suffering, both the public's expectations and his professional oath, which shape his own conception of his role, require that he keep the patient alive and "hope for the best." Nevertheless, this dominant position and unrealistic optimism when death is inevitable make it extremely difficult for him to relinquish this role and prepare the patient and family for the imminent death. Beyond the boundary of his capacity to relieve suffering, the doctor must choose an appropriate course in an area uncharted by traditional guidelines. Whether he attempts to avoid or to make these decisions, he and those who accept this responsibility with him are threatened with uncertainty and by their own fears in the presence of death.

Pertinent norms for terminal decisions are absolutely essential if the medical profession is to cope realistically with this problem. The urgency of the task of formulating such guidelines is reflected both by the difficulty with which these decisions are now made, or avoided, and by the large and rapidly expanding aged population. In 1972 the number of people in the United States past the age of sixty-five was more than six times the number in 1900 and totaled over 20,000,000.[2] Because of this increase, we can expect the number of people who will die each year to double within the next decade. The need for adequate norms to confront the problems of terminal illness is further underscored by the rising number of deaths from cancer and major cardiovascular and renal diseases, which are often accompanied by some degree of suffering. In order to discover an adequate basis for resolving the questions that arise in the context of caring for the terminally ill and the fatally injured, it is necessary to examine the medical problems and the alternatives that are available. Furthermore, it is necessary to interpret and relate the values that have traditionally informed the art of medicine to the dilemmas created by the science of medicine. It is only within this context that the controversy over the practice of euthanasia can be resolved satisfactorily.

ALTERNATIVES WITHIN
CONTEMPORARY MEDICINE

The therapeutic resources of the medical profession are far too numerous to permit a comprehensive summary of the drugs and techniques applicable to the diverse contingencies of critical injury and illness. Nevertheless, for the purposes of analysis they can be divided into the following categories according to the primary purposes for which they are employed, and representative examples of each can be cited. It should be observed at the outset, however, that many procedures can be directed toward more than one objective and can be prescribed with more than one end in view and thus may be included within several of these categories:

1. *Preventive therapy* serves to avert illness and injury by attacking their causes and by building and supplementing natural resistance. Such procedures include vitamins, immunizations, and antibiotics. Other preventive measures that are directly related to the following modes of treatment consist of the highly sophisticated monitoring devices that permit impending crises to be detected and in many cases avoided.

2. *Emergency therapy*, which is immediately put into effect, involves such first-aid procedures as artificial respiration, blood transfusions, heart massage, stimulants, and renal dialysis. Their primary function is to restore or replace vital functions in order to "buy" time until more adequate treatment is available or until the doctor can determine the exact nature of the problem and institute appropriate measures.

3. *Remedial therapy* is applied after diagnosis and is

directed toward the sources of difficulty. Treatment within this category includes the use of antibiotics, chemotherapy, radiation, and a broad range of surgical procedures that are prescribed and performed for the purpose of correcting abnormality, healing injury, and curing disease.

4. *Ameliorative therapy* consists of those measures which are not directed toward cure *per se* but are supportive and often treat the symptoms rather than the sources of disorder. Hormones, protein supplements, electrolytes, radiation, blood transfusions, artificial respirators, pacemakers, and renal dialysis are employed in order to improve and to supplement essential organic functions. Their basic purpose is to complement or serve in the place of therapy within the other categories.

5. *Palliative therapy* is also directed toward the relief of symptoms and is closely related to the mode of treatment used for ameliorative therapy. It includes the use of numerous anesthetics, analgesic agents, radiation, neurosurgery, and psychotherapeutic treatment, which serve to alleviate pain and mitigate both the physical and the emotional suffering that accompany illness and injury. These measures are pursued in conjunction with other forms of therapy and in their absence when, for example, they are inadequate, unfeasible, or unavailable.

On the basis of his training and experience and often in consultation with other physicians, a doctor determines which of the available alternatives are appropriate to the requirements of each case. The total program of care that he prescribes may include measures within several of these categories and on different levels within each. As conditions

change, a constant vigilance has to be maintained in order
that therapy can be adjusted in accordance with the
changing requirements. Such choices and adjustments are
relatively simple in the majority of cases when prognosis is
good and the patient responds well to treatment. They
become extremely problematical in critical cases and when
the patient fails to respond and his condition deteriorates.
Then therapy may include highly sophisticated procedures
in all five categories, especially in modern intensive care
units. Furthermore, it may go beyond the so-called standard practices and involve experimental measures directed
toward the objectives of one or more of these categories.
While not restricted to critical cases, relatively unproven
and unestablished measures are often employed when
standard techniques of emergency, remedial, ameliorative,
or palliative therapy are not effective. In such cases, they
take the form of desperate, last-resort efforts to prolong life
or relieve suffering.

AT THE END OF
OUR TECHNOLOGICAL TETHER

The problem of determining the proper scope and
objectives of medical care becomes even more complex
when the condition of the victim of injury or disease is
diagnosed as incurable and all the means of remedial
therapy are exhausted without success. It becomes especially difficult when emergency and ameliorative procedures
make possible only a severely restricted level of existence,
such that the patient suffers in spite of intense palliative
therapy or his life is suspended in a state of unconsciousness.
The numerous questions that must be resolved in the
context of these cases include at least the following:

1. Should remedial procedures be terminated and
only other forms of therapy be pursued?

2. What level of treatment constitutes "good" medicine within each of the remaining categories in relation to the circumstances of each case?

3. Should therapy be restricted to merely palliative and limited forms of ameliorative procedures in order for the patient to die "from natural causes"?

4. Should palliative measures be intensified that not only would relieve suffering but would hasten the patient's death?

Obviously no invariable rules can be created to answer these questions and to assure every patient adequate relief. The needs and conditions of dying patients are far too diverse, and in spite of dramatic progress within all branches of medical science, our understanding of suffering is still too limited. Each case must be analyzed individually, but there are several general observations with regard to human suffering that should inform decisions.

Whatever may be isolated as its specific cause, suffering is always both psychological and physiological. Its relief depends upon careful attention to both of these dimensions. Physical pain is often one of the basic components of suffering, especially in cases of severe illness and injury, but pain is a highly subjective phenomenon. Different persons perceive and react to it differently, and the experience of pain usually varies for the same person at different times. In the last analysis, as Dr. Richard I. H. Wang has observed, "real knowledge of the quality and behavior of a pain . . . belongs only to the one who experiences the pain." [3]

Anxiety and depression are usually regarded as emotional components of suffering, but they are intimately related to physical pain. On the one hand, feelings of apprehension, depression, and anxiety often exaggerate the experience of pain. On the other hand, pain is also emotionally destructive. In terminal cases, it tends to create an awareness of the possibility of death, and this frequently causes or increases depression, but pain is also much more directly connected with emotional suffering. As Dr. J. M. Hinton has observed, "anxiety and depression are closely related to both the duration of illness and the intensity of physical distress." [4] In short, "a prolonged and intense bombardment of the central nervous system may lead to severe mental depression, personality disorganization, and complete abolition of the pleasure of living and the fear of dying." [5]

Although an appropriate program of terminal care depends upon many aspects of the patient's personality and experience, symptomatic relief of pain is always crucial in order to alleviate his suffering. Management of acute pain can usually be accomplished by nonspecific supportive measures or by definitive therapy directed toward its underlying causes. Chronic pain, however, is usually a much more difficult and time-consuming problem. Furthermore, the results are likely to be disappointing both to the patient and to the physician. Often there is no specific therapy that is altogether effective, and sometimes the patient's psychological reactions toward pain further complicate treatment.[6]

For patients with incurable but not directly fatal conditions, successful control of severe and unrelenting pain is especially problematic, because synthetic analgesic drugs are often insufficient, narcotic analgesics are addicting, and neurosurgical procedures usually have serious side effects. Such chronic and intractable pain, however, occurs far less frequently in conditions of nonmalignant etiology than in cases of advanced cancer. When remedial therapy fails to eradicate malignancy and ameliorative measures cease to provide adequate relief, palliative treatment, which is intensified as the disease advances, sometimes requires large dosages of potent narcotics in order to control pain. In such cases, the problem of addiction is relatively insignificant in comparison with the benefits of these analgesics; nevertheless, all narcotic drugs tend to cause other undesirable side effects, including respiratory depression, nausea, constipation, and vomiting.[7] These must be evaluated carefully in order to alleviate the patient's suffering. Neurosurgical intervention is often preferred, for even when narcotized to the point of sleep, many patients are never entirely free of pain.[8] Radical neurosurgical procedures, however, are usually deferred until life expectancy is limited to a year or less because of their serious secondary effects.[9] The policy recommended by Dr. Guy Owens, chief of the Department of Neurosurgery at Roswell Park Memorial Institute, is "to describe the various procedures in detail to the patient including the undesirable but often-observed side effects. If he can then ask for help with full understanding of the undesired costs, we find a usually highly satisfied person after surgery." [10] But what of the patient who cannot and will not "ask for help" when he fully understands the "costs" ? Should he be offered another option: the choice to die—rather than either to continue to endure pain that is only temporarily and partially relieved or to submit to unwanted surgical procedures for relief?

Appropriate treatment of the dying requires not only that the problem of suffering be taken into account but also that the complex phenomenon of death be understood. Much of the confusion and indecision in response to the crucial questions that must be resolved in the context of these cases stems both from the inadequacy of our traditional conceptions of death and from our inability to accept its reality. It is therefore necessary to come to grips with both of these issues in order to make responsible decisions in each case and in order to contribute to the formulation of suitable guidelines for terminal decisions in general.

In the first place, there are at least two kinds, or levels, of death: organismic or somatic death, the death of the body as a whole, and organic or cellular death, the death of the component parts of the body. When the former occurs, that is, when circulatory and respiratory and other vital functions cease, the individual cells of the body begin to degenerate at rapid but unequal rates. Although some organs have a greater capacity to withstand and recover from a relatively prolonged period without oxygen, the central nervous system is most vulnerable and suffers irreparable damage after only approximately four minutes. Thus organic death may take the form of "cerebral" death which can be caused by a number of conditions, such as cardiac arrest, occlusive stroke, spontaneous hypoglycemia, carbon monoxide, and other forms of poisoning that deprive the brain of the necessary oxygen and other metabolites carried in the blood cells.

We usually conceive of death in terms of the first definition, as the absence of vital organic functions. But this index has been rendered obsolete as a basis for terminal decisions by the innovations in medical technology that have made preventive, emergency, and ameliorative procedures extremely effective. The interruption of respiration, for instance, is no longer regarded as a sign of death but rather as a signal for the initiation of resuscitative techniques. The cessation of heartbeat has become a frequently manageable medical syndrome known as cardiac arrest, which calls for the immediate administration of stimulants and heart massage.[11] With the aid of sensitive monitoring devices, potential failures can often be detected and averted. By means of the numerous organ supplements and substitutes within the scope of ameliorative therapy, vital functions can be sustained artificially for prolonged periods.

Certain procedures can make dramatic recoveries possible in many cases that once would have been considered hopeless. But because organismic death and organic death do not occur simultaneously, these procedures can be employed with tragic consequences. When they are applied or continued after the central nervous system has become nonviable, they serve only "to maintain the look of life in the face of death while agonizing and expensive prolongation of false hope continues for all concerned." [12] Such cases often result from the limitations of our customary understanding of death as merely the absence of essential biological functions. On this basis, a patient can be regarded as technically alive so long as these vital processes continue, whether spontaneously or artificially. The doctor, since he is obligated to preserve human life, is often considered responsible for its care. Appropriate terminal decisions could be made with much less difficulty if human life were understood to include at least the potentiality for consciousness and if death were recognized when the physical substratum for this level of existence has been destroyed or has degenerated.

In the second place, however, death cannot be understood nor can responsible medical decisions be made solely from a biological point of view. Although death is an event and a state that can be analyzed and described in biochemical and physiological terms, it is also, as Dr. Charles W. Wahl points out, "a complex symbol, the significance of which will vary from one person to another and from one culture to another." [13] The principal symbols concerning death in contemporary American society are the products of a pattern of avoidance that is reflected in the practice of transferring the duties and ceremonies surrounding the event of death to professional functionaries trained and paid to regard it impersonally. On the one hand, this way of "managing" death is indicative of our inability to come to terms with its reality. On the other hand, our interpretation of its meaning and our inability to cope with it are profoundly shaped and restricted by this pervasive effort to disguise and to deny it.

In the context of terminal cases, our petty euphemisms, desperate hopes for a "new cure," and even our objective scientific terminology only partially veil its threatening proximity. The entire episode surrounding death is characteristically a crisis for all concerned. For the terminal patient, death is primarily an intrapersonal crisis, and everything related to his dying is significant only insofar as it impinges on his own experience of this process. Insecure in an unfamiliar environment, he often feels a loss of dignity and self-control and experiences a sense of shame because of his extreme dependence. His anxiety is intensified by insufficiently relieved and inadequately explained physical symptoms. He becomes susceptible to extreme loneliness and depression, "the bereavement of the dying," [14] when deprived of significant emotional support and attachments by the overindulgent isolation frequently imposed by the living. Furthermore, customary defenses against the threat of death are undermined as physical and emotional suffering continue and the patient becomes increasingly aware of its imminence.

Reactions in the face of death seem to vary widely. As Dr. Arnold A. Hutschnecker has observed, the responsive attitudes of most dying patients toward their environment and their mental and physical behavior patterns remain more or less consistent with their previous attitudes and actions.[15] For many the recognition that death is personally near may be quite different from the perception of it from a temporal distance. The elderly and especially those in poor health often develop rather well organized, positive, forward-looking attitudes toward death.[16] By those who are able to accept its reality in this manner, death may be regarded as a release. For others, death remains a threat which they consistently suppress beneath the level of consciousness. When confronted with its inevitability, these patients tend to erect pathological defenses of denial, revenge, or suicide. The majority, however, meet the crisis of death with vacillating and conflicting responses between these extremes. Too broken in body and spirit to wish desperately to live, they often have a positive motivation toward death. Yet, because they are fearful and threatened both by the event and by their own half-conscious desire to die, they cling to life and grasp for vague hopes of recovery.[17]

For the family of the dying, death is a crisis with complex intrapersonal and interpersonal dimensions that are significantly influenced by cultural values, practices, and institutions. In the first place, the death of another frequently foreshadows that of all who are present, and the fear of death is often greater among the living than it is for the dying. The inability of relatives to cope with this threat is one of the prime reasons for their denial of the reality of death, even when it is imminent. In the second place, the "small family system" in our society tends to give rise to strong and involved affective relationships which contribute to this crisis. In the intimate family circle, bonds of love, dependence, and identification are so reinforced that the death of a member is experienced as a seemingly irreplaceable loss. Also within this context, orientations of ambivalence and hostility are generated, and death creates profound feelings of guilt. In addition to the fear of dying, such responses of grief, sorrow, shame, and guilt contribute to the denial of death and make it extremely difficult for the family to come to terms with the dying and share the responsibility of determining the proper terminal care for one of its number.

Reinforced by the optimism and avoidance of death by society in general, this denial intensifies the crisis that inevitably results when death occurs and makes emotional

adjustments extremely difficult. Further, while our cultural
expectations and prescribed roles for the bereaved emphasize and often assuage feelings of loss and grief, they do not
adequately provide for release and replacement when these
needs are strong, nor do they make real provisions for other
emotional and personal needs, such as hostility and grief
and their displacement or discharge. Those who experience
acute grief, according to Dr. Erich Lindemann, often search
during the time before death for evidence of failure to do
right by the lost one, accuse themselves of negligence and
exaggerate minor omissions, and tend to respond with
irritability and anger.[18] Their hostility may be spread out
over all their relationships, but it may also be directed
toward specific persons and is sometimes expressed in bitter
criticism of the doctor. While they usually do not take
action against him, as a truly paranoid person might, they
characteristically talk a great deal about their suspicions.[19]
This dimension of the crisis of death for the family also
makes the question of their participation in terminal
decisions especially problematic.

Finally, death is difficult and a multifaceted crisis for the
doctor. In the first place, he is related to patients in their
most profound physical and emotional need and is responsible for the application of suitable therapeutic measures. He
therefore must make sure that every reasonable effort has
been made to bring about their recovery and that they
remain as free of pain as possible. He must also "help the
patient achieve an appropriate emotional world in which to
die." [20] In the second place, he is related to the members of
the family of the terminal patient and is responsible for
preparing them prior to death in order that they may be
able to understand and give support to the dying person,
may participate in the making of critical decisions with
regard to his care, and may cope with their own suffering
and loss after death has occurred. The way in which the

physician fulfills these responsibilities depends in large measure on his ability to manage the interpersonal and intrapersonal crises of death.

Adequate medical care for the terminally ill is often demanding and frustrating. In their anxiety, many patients become extremely difficult and tend to alienate themselves from the doctor's interest and sympathy. Their dying may arouse his own fear of death and stimulate reactions of avoidance that result in their being rejected, at least as persons. Many physicians, for example, acquire a "professional" attitude of not becoming "personally involved" and attempt to treat death as an impersonal event, stripped of all human dimensions.[21] In some cases, their denial of its reality takes the form of elaborate, heroic measures and frantic maneuvers applied in desperation in the very face of death. Not unlike the public in general, they frequently try to make it less real and less threatening by referring to death euphemistically.

The doctor's reluctance to admit "defeat" and his inability to help the patient and the family come to grips with death are often reinforced by their own efforts to avoid its reality. In many cases, his own conception of himself and of his competence is shaped both by their unrealistic confidence in his ability to avert disaster and by the role he assumes in order to relieve their fear and anxiety. When death supervenes, however, the physician's defenses against the threat of death can be weakened, and because of his countertransference, he may become susceptible to feelings of disillusionment and failure. Furthermore, he also becomes vulnerable to accusations of neglect and foul play from those who feel guilty over their relationships with the deceased. In order to resolve their individual intrapersonal crises and to protect his own reputation, the doctor must often be able to convince the family and himself that they did "everything possible" for the patient.

THE CONTEXT OF TERMINAL
MEDICAL PRACTICE

Appropriate terminal care has to be determined in each case with reference to the specific needs of the dying patient and the alternatives that are available with which to meet his needs. Nevertheless, moral norms including professional and legal requirements for medical practice are necessary for the protection of both patients and doctors. Moral standards and rules of practice must take into account the diverse conditions that call for difficult life and death decisions. Such moral norms also have to take into consideration the social structures in which these decisions must be made. Therefore, in order to evaluate current standards of terminal medical practice from an ethical perspective, it is essential to understand the moral questions that confront doctors and the demands and expectations of society, which have an important bearing on the way in which these questions are interpreted and resolved.

The Medical Context of Terminal Decisions

There are especially difficult questions to resolve when a terminal patient experiences pain that is only partially relieved. In cases of cancer, for example, after every available form of remedial therapy has failed to effect remission or check its spread, decisions frequently have to be made with regard to the application of measures that will only temporarily postpone death. Should the physician, on the one hand, continue to employ every possible means to maintain the patient's life even at the expense of his suffering or by rendering him permanently unconscious? Or, on the other hand, should he terminate supportive procedures and administer narcotics sufficient to alleviate suffering, even at the expense of the patient's life?

The array of problems that arise in dealing with an unconscious patient is no less complex even when the patient has no apparent chance of recovery. What constitutes good medical practice for the victim of radical brain damage as the result of a severe hemorrhage or an automobile accident? What are the doctor's responsibilities in cases of cardiac arrest when emergency resuscitation techniques reestablish and sustain vital functions after the brain has been anoxic too long? Once these measures are introduced, is he obligated to maintain them indefinitely? Is there a distinction between terminating the procedures by which a patient's life is sustained and terminating his life, when the latter is a necessary consequence of the former?

On delivering an irremediably malformed infant, a doctor may be faced with the choice of either refusing to aspirate the child in order to permit it to die or to aspirate it even though the child will live for only a few months or years at a severely restricted level of existence and at extreme emotional and financial expense to the parents. If he chooses to aspirate, or if breathing is spontaneous, he then must determine the level of therapy to be applied. Should he attempt to prolong the infant's life by whatever means necessary, or should he administer only "routine" care and allow it to die?

Questions that are equally difficult arise in the context of terminal medical care of the aged. Conditions requiring life and death decisions range from acute diseases, such as cancer and cardiovascular conditions, which are more frequent among the elderly, to chronic diseases that are complicated by the general systemic degeneration of the aging process. In cases involving these conditions, should doctors do everything possible to prolong life, or should the old and dying be allowed to die in peace? The growing number of geriatric patients who require life-sustaining treatment underscores the importance of relevant criteria for determining appropriate care.

The problems of terminal medical practice are far too complex to permit all the uncertainties and conflicting arguments to be resolved easily. Furthermore, we cannot expect that scientific progress alone will relieve our confusion. In all probability, we shall perfect techniques of resuscitation and of life support to such an extent that it will become virtually impossible for an aged, disease-torn, or hopelessly damaged body to die until we decide that it should. The implications of this growing power over death are not fully comprehended by many who are responsible for its use.

The Social Context of Terminal Decisions

To understand the practice of medicine in terminal cases, it is necessary to examine the pattern of private practice in our society. This is the conventional perspective from which the structure, standards, and expectations of medical care are defined. The classic doctor-patient relationship constitutes the central unit in this approach to medical practice. An examination of this relationship provides insight into the way in which both doctors and patients interpret their respective roles. It is especially important to note the way in which this relationship functions in the context of terminal cases. In this connection, it is useful to refer to a typology of relationships between physicians and patients developed by Szasz and Hollender. In a study reported in the *Archives of Internal Medicine* in 1956, they delineate three basic models for interpreting interpersonal and therapeutic relationships between physicians and patients. These models are: activity-passivity, guidance-cooperation, and mutual participation. Each is said to be necessary and appropriate for particular circumstances.[22]

The model of mutual participation is based on the essential equality of persons and corresponds with the social structure of democracy. Interaction on this level is often desired by the patient, is generally characterized by greater empathy, and is "realistic" and necessary in some circumstances, especially in chronic illness. In this context the physician does not decide for the patient the proper course to follow but helps the patient to help himself. Although this orientation is essentially foreign to medicine, it expresses the way in which the doctor-patient relationship is usually regarded by society.

It is important to note that this model explains the financial and legal relationship between doctors and patients. It might be described as a capitalistic model in which the doctor is understood as the performer of medical "services" and the patient, who is in need of these services, as the employer who engages him. If members of professions should be considered as small "entrepreneurs" rather than as employees, doctors can be compared with merchants or producers of "goods" and "services" and the patient can be thought of as the "customer" who purchases them. Talcott Parsons points out that "this paradigm is so deeply ingrained in our cultural heritage that it is not surprising that it should be generalized to the professional level and 'the doctor' as an individual be thought of as set over against the patient." [23]

The guidance-cooperation model underlies much of medical practice and suggests that the relationship between patient and physician is analogous to that between parent and child. The doctor is given, or assumes, the primary responsibility by virtue of his greater knowledge. Although the patient has aspirations and feelings of his own, he is expected to "look up to" and to "obey" his doctor. Both the

doctor and the patient, however, contribute to the relationship and participate actively in therapy, but in this model
the physician tends to identify less with the patient as a
person than in the previous orientation. This pattern is said
to be appropriate when the patient is more seriously ill and
is willing to "cooperate" with the doctor.

The activity-passivity model is indicative of the doctor-
patient relationship that underlies the application of some of
the more advanced techniques and practices of medical
science. In this frame of reference, the doctor's orientation
toward his patient is somewhat analogous to a parent's
relationship to an infant; that is, he is active and in control
of the situation while the patient is passive and helpless.
This is said to be appropriate for the treatment of emergencies, for example, when the patient is severely injured,
bleeding, delirious, or in a coma. Strictly speaking, there is
little or no interrelation in this model, "because it is based
on the effect of one person on another in such a way and in
such circumstances that the person acted upon is unable to
contribute actively, or is considered to be inanimate." [24]
"Agreement" concerning what is best for the patient is
taken for granted by the physician, and "treatment" is
determined and pursued regardless of the patient's contribution and in spite of the outcome.

•

THE CONDUCT OF TERMINAL MEDICAL CARE

Terminal medical care can best be understood on the
basis of the activity-passivity model. For emotional and
professional reasons, doctors tend to avoid becoming personally involved with dying patients. Although it requires
that they accept a greater burden of responsibility, doctors
usually assume a primary role in the doctor-patient relationship. In many cases, terminal patients are not able to

comprehend their condition and cannot participate in decisions concerning their care. Even when their patients are able to make responsible decisions, however, doctors generally prefer an "activity-passivity" relationship in terminal cases. This orientation is reflected, for example, in an editorial by Dr. J. Russell Elkinton, editor of the *Annals of Internal Medicine*. Dr. Elkinton acknowledges that it is often difficult to judge what constitutes the quality of life for a particular patient and thus to decide the proper therapeutic course to follow; nevertheless, he concludes that this "must lie with the conscience of the physician." [25]

A patient's prognosis is a crucial component of responsible medical decisions. The most remote glimmer of "hope" and occasional "miraculous" recoveries tend to redouble the physician's resolve to employ every available measure. This determination is often warranted, especially by the resilience of youth, but it can also become radically unrealistic as an inflexible standard in the treatment of the elderly. When injury or disease or involutional changes of senescence eliminate every chance of recovery, some other goal must be chosen and with it another standard as a basis for choosing a means of medical care. This, of course, does not necessarily mean the end of all hope, either for the patient or for those close to him. Medical science, although bereft of its power to heal, can still "buy time"—a short or prolonged, welcomed or endured reprieve from death. Under what circumstances should life-sustaining measures be employed in terminal cases involving geriatric patients, and when should they be removed? Our ability to resolve this perplexing moral problem in the exercise of our technical ability often determines whether the living and the dying are able to redeem some meaning from death or are rendered hopeless by its presence.

The difficulties of terminal medical care seem to be widely recognized. Furthermore, there is a basic consensus

within our society that the value or "sanctity" of life
constitutes the starting point of medical ethics. Nevertheless, the implications of this principle are no longer clear,
especially in relation to the extensive control that doctors
are able to exercise over life and death. Many people
interpret the "sanctity of life" to mean that life *per se* is of
ultimate significance. They conclude that doctors should
secure the maximum longevity possible in every case. Some
doctors also believe that their fundamental obligation is to
preserve life. They insist that this responsibility does not
change in difficult cases and is not altered by their new
knowledge and skills. Dr. Charles S. Cameron, for example,
states this position:

> It is not the privilege of any doctor to decide that he should
> shorten life. The preservation of life must be the sole
> principle guiding medical practice, including the treatment
> of the hopeless cancer patient. This principle cannot be
> tampered with or interpreted loosely.[26]

From Dr. Cameron's perspective, the difference between
euthanasia and letting the patient die by omitting life-sustaining treatment is a moral quibble. Essentially the same
argument is made by Dr. David Karnofsky of New York's
Sloan-Kettering Institute:

> The patient entrusts his life to his doctor, and it is the
> doctor's duty to sustain it as long as it is possible. There
> should be no suggestion that it is possible for the doctor to do
> otherwise, even if it were decided that the patient were
> "better off dead." [27]

There are a number of physicians, however, who disagree
with this position. From their point of view, biological
existence is not the only or even the most important
dimension of human life. Doctors who judge the value of
life in relation to its quality seek primarily to secure their

patients' physical and emotional well-being and to relieve their suffering. They tend to work with the assumption that every doctor has to do the best for his patient, even if this should occasionally mean turning a blind eye to general rules. Implicit in this approach to terminal medical care is the recognition that a doctor's responsibility for a patient's life is limited by his responsibility to the patient as a person.

Insight into the extent of this divergence of opinion is provided by a survey of American doctors which was published in the *New Medical Materia* in 1962. In the first place, 31.2 percent of the doctors surveyed approved of active euthanasia for cases in which "the patient is in great pain, and there is no hope of recovery." Classified according to religion, the figures were: Protestants 38.5 percent, Catholics 6.7 percent, Jews 38.8 percent. In the second place, 32.8 percent approved of active euthanasia for cases in which "an infant, born with serious abnormalities, has no chance of normal life." Classified according to religion, the figures were: Protestants 40.7 percent, Catholics 6.2 percent, Jews 40.8 percent. In the third place, 39.6 percent favored the practice of active euthanasia when safeguarded by a requirement that "more than one doctor must certify the hopelessness of the situation." Finally, 80.8 percent of the doctors who opposed active euthanasia indicated that passive euthanasia, "letting the patient die," might be justified in some cases.[28]

In a 1968 survey of 418 staff physicians in a university hospital and a community hospital in Seattle, Washington, 72 percent indicated that they approved of negative euthanasia under certain conditions; 40 percent favored a signed statement authorizing negative euthanasia; and 59 percent indicated that they would practice negative euthanasia with such a statement. In the same survey, 31 percent favored social changes to permit positive euthanasia, and 28 percent indicated that they would practice positive euthanasia if social attitudes permitted.[29] A somewhat more conservative attitude toward active (i.e., positive) euthanasia is reflected in a similar survey of professors of medicine reported by Dr. Robert H. Williams. As a basis for his presidential address before the Association of American Physicians in 1969, Williams sent questionnaires to members of both the Association of Professors of Medicine and the Association of American Physicians. Of the 344 responses, only 15 percent favored positive euthanasia; 87 percent, however, favored negative euthanasia, and 80 percent indicated that they had practiced it.[30]

It is, perhaps, impossible to determine how often doctors share or assume the responsibility for making terminal decisions. The "conspiracy of silence" that surrounds death threatens with misunderstanding those who would openly attempt to come to grips with the dilemmas that arise in caring for the dying. Even when passive (i.e., negative) euthanasia is practiced, it is usually performed discreetly "at that nebulous point where the family reinforces the physician's feeling that 'we have done all we can.' " [31] It may take the form of a doctor's order for the attending nurses not to call in case of an "emergency" or a decision to place the patient on a lower level of therapy. Dr. Charles K. Hofling suggests that, when the patient's standing in the community is inconspicuous, the decision to suspend vital treatment may be made by the physician-in-charge without consultation with the family, and in most nondenominational hospitals the decision is most often made without consulting clergymen or lawyers.[32] An example of this practice is described by Dr. John H. Isaacs, an associate professor at Loyola University's Stritch School of Medicine:

> One patient of mine obviously had terminal carcinoma with metastasis. I undertook heroic measures because she was a personal friend. I felt she could be maintained reasonably

well for another month if I gave her the exact amount of fluid she needed and checked the electrolytes every two or three days. But after 10 days or so it became obvious that what I was doing was utter nonsense. I didn't discuss things with the family. They saw the I.V. fluids going, but I reduced the 3,500 or 4,800 c.c. of dextrose and water to 1,000 c.c. run slowly over a 24-hour period. In a few days the patient succumbed to her disease and to electrolyte imbalance and dehydration. The family didn't have to make the decision. I'd made it. I hadn't burdened them with the decision because they were close friends of mine, and I know that this was morally acceptable.[33]

In many cases, the physician has virtually no alternative but to assume the full responsibility for prescribing terminal care. When the patient is either unconscious or emotionally unable to accept and to respond to his dying, the doctor is denied a primary insight into the proper course to follow. When the patient's family are not able to acknowledge the inevitability of his death and to overcome their grief and guilt, they cannot share the burden of decision. Furthermore, if a doctor practices in an area in which his colleagues believe it to be their duty to preserve life as long as possible regardless of how hopeless the patient's condition, he may be deprived of consultation with other doctors.

SLIPPING THE HORNS OF THE DILEMMA

Stated in its simplest terms, the dilemma that confronts the doctor in difficult terminal cases is as follows: If he decides to prolong a patient's life as long as possible, there is a danger of destroying the value of life by causing useless suffering. Furthermore, there is a risk of creating emotional and financial hardships for the family. If he chooses to allow or to cause a patient to die, there is a danger of violating the sanctity of life or of undermining the value of life as an ethical principle. There is also the risk of error and of professional and legal censure. This dilemma exposes a cross section of the values underlying professional medical ethics and the norms and expectations of society. It is not resolved by paying lip service to a set of moral standards while performing or passively condoning acts that contradict these norms. Constructive efforts to "slip the horns" of this dilemma require an examination of basic ethical values and a reappraisal of the implications of these principles in the light of the problems of terminal medical care.

It is especially important to discover or to create a consensus on the level of ethical values as a basis for moral norms and policies for terminal decisions. Anxiety and fear of death account for the failure of both the medical profession and society in general to grasp the potentially demonic consequences of useless extension of life, on the one hand, and of furtive, *ad hoc* decisions to "release" the sufferer, on the other. Therefore, in order to establish policies with which to avoid these dangers, it is necessary to foster a more healthy and realistic orientation toward death. One major task is to define "death" and set up appropriate criteria for determining when death occurs. This requires that a number of factual considerations be taken into account. In the last analysis, however, a definition of such a controversial and indeterminate term is primarily "persuasive" or "practical" rather than descriptive. Consequently, basic ethical principles have a significant bearing on the way "death" is defined. Because it is normative, a definition of "death" has a decisive influence on policies and decisions concerning the use of emergency and ameliorative treatment.

To overcome the dilemma that arises in the context of terminal medical care, it is also important to change the basic structure of medical practice. Balanced and responsible decisions among the numerous alternatives and their consequences in the practice of contemporary medicine often require a more comprehensive perspective than that provided by the traditional pattern of private practice. This orientation is adequate for cases in which illness or injury is not acute or is manageable by routine and relatively inexpensive therapy. Nevertheless, it is frequently insufficient to meet the demands of serious cases in which the risks are high, treatment is expensive, or knowledge and techniques are uncertain or limited. In the first place, it places too much responsibility on the physician. When he cannot cure, he becomes vulnerable to criticism, whether he chooses to prolong life as long as possible or determines to employ merely palliative treatment and "let nature take its course." In the second place, it threatens to exclude from consideration legitimate needs and desires of the patient, as well as those of his relatives. Thus it tends to undermine his freedom and dignity. In the third place, private practice often confines medical decisions within the boundaries of the doctor-patient relationship. In so doing, it fails to take into account the multitude of limitations and responsibilities that impinge on it and have important bearings on the choices that are made. Because of this limitation, many complex problems, including those created by the increasing expense of medical care, by the shortage of technical personnel and facilities, as well as those arising from extensive prolongation of life, appear to be insoluble.

Commitment to established patterns of thought and action tends to impose blinders on our minds and to restrict our ability to respond imaginatively to new and difficult situations. Proposals for change produce a sense of uneasiness and are often misunderstood. Responsible medical decisions especially in terminal cases require standards and structures that are sensitive to a broad spectrum of human needs and responsive to the claims and desires of both the patient and those intimately related to him. The inadequacy of traditional professional norms of medical practice and the obsolescence of the classical doctor-patient relationship make it necessary to find new alternatives. The purpose of the following chapter is to examine the dilemma of terminal medical decisions from a legal perspective. In the concluding chapter, specific guidelines are suggested for moral and legal norms with which to resolve the dilemma.

5

THE LETTER OF THE LAW
AND THE SPIRIT OF MERCY

Most of the decisions of the physician appear to be free
from legal restraint and compulsion. Even in the areas in
which he seems to be legally free, however, he is not
altogether at liberty to conduct himself as he chooses.
Societal expectations and professional norms have a profound influence on his actions. These controls are often
more effective than the legal structure in regulating his
behavior. They also exert tremendous pressure on courts
and legislatures and thus determine the legally acceptable
level of medical practice. The serious dilemmas that the
doctor confronts as a result of our scientific and technological innovations are therefore not simply matters of personal
morals or merely questions of medical ethics. They are, at
the same time, problems that are inextricably connected
with the law.

Insofar as the question of euthanasia is concerned, the
standards of the medical profession and those of our legal
system are essentially the same. They are products of the
same moral tradition and complement each other at this
point. At least in theory, both reject active euthanasia as an
acceptable medical practice. In fact, however, the ambivalence with which the physician sometimes chooses between
conflicting needs and values in the face of suffering and

death is reflected in the administration of the law and the application of its sanctions. When decisions are required, neither medical standards nor legal norms are followed with consistency. Consequently, an understanding of the legal dimensions of euthanasia requires not only a recognition of the substantive principles of our criminal law but also an awareness of the nature, purpose, and limitations of law in general and of the extralegal principles that control decisions in the context of difficult cases.

THE NATURE AND SOURCE OF LAW

The way in which "law" is defined often reflects more about the lexicographer than about the subject. To minimize this problem, it is necessary to take into account the more proximate sources and functions of the law rather than to join in the classical debate over its ultimate ground or essence. Whatever may be regarded as the source of its authority, whether the law be derived from divine revelation, right reason, or secular power, its requirements are created by human choices in response to human needs and values. Together these decisions form a human institution that orders society and resolves conflicts on the basis of the accumulated wisdom and experience of the past. As such, neither the system nor its norms is sacrosanct. To be relevant to changing circumstances, both must be evaluated and amended constantly. This flexibility is built into the common-law tradition, for although its precedents and statutes objectify what must and what must not be done, considerable leeway is permitted in their interpretation and application.

The typology with which Henry David Aiken distinguishes between four fundamentally different levels of moral discourse serves as an instructive tool for examining the scope and interests of the law in relation to morality. In contrast with spontaneous, emotional expressions on the "expressive-evocative" level, appeal to law and the procedures involved in its application tend to be more logical and impersonal. They operate primarily on the "moral" level of reasoning. Like codes of professional or business ethics, legal rules and principles serve as the criteria by which specific problems are resolved and conduct is evaluated. This process, however, is not one of formal logic, nor is it controlled solely by principles of legality. In the absence of relevant "legal" norms, judicial decisions frequently solve controversies and assign responsibilities on the basis of general, *prima facie* moral obligations, such as the duty to keep promises, to prevent injustice, to prolong life, and to prevent unnecessary suffering. These decisions are as authoritative as those derived from more "legal" norms, and in many cases they are regarded as landmark decisions in the law.[1]

In spite of their interdependence, there are important differences between law and morality. At least two significant points of contrast provide insight into the way the problem of euthanasia is understood from each perspective. In the first place, on the "moral" level of normative reasoning, moral norms are far more comprehensive than legal rules in the range of their interests and applicability. In the second place, on the "ethical" level, there are principles and values that altogether transcend the moral and legal norms with reference to which the law functions. These ethical principles constitute the bases for evaluating and affirming or amending moral codes and legal requirements.

On the strictly "moral" level of normative reasoning, morality attends not only to the entire spectrum of human behavior but also to intimately related feelings, beliefs, and values. In comparison with other moral norms, legal standards tend to be concerned primarily with specific, overt actions and omissions. Even though legal standards are often derived from moral principles, the law cannot always translate the interests of morality directly into legal terms. Its requirements often constitute a minimal ethic; therefore, decisions and conduct based solely on what is legal are not always morally good or desirable. Even legal standards which are usually necessary and just can cause suffering and injustice in some circumstances, especially when they are applied too literally.

Since no law can cover all situations, as needs vary and conditions change, legal norms must be interpreted and applied accordingly. Throughout this process the law cannot avoid dealing with the subjective motivations and intentions that prompt behavior. In fact, according to its traditional meaning, and the view commonly expressed by judges, the "act" to which law directs its attention includes the "volition" that precedes or accompanies and causes action.[2] Although difficult to assess and harder to prove, motives must be taken into account in order to assign responsibility and liability. Civil law therefore establishes specific "defenses," and criminal law provides certain "excuses" and "justifications" on the basis of which legal guilt, like moral guilt, may vary in accordance with mental attitude. Some crimes, such as assault and homicide, are divided into degrees or species dependent upon motive, purpose, or intent.[3] Theoretically, the law is interested only in determining the *presence* or the *absence* of motive and intent rather than in deciding whether or not they are morally acceptable. In reality, however, moral as well as legal judgments enter into deliberations with regard to the application of these distinctions.

On the "ethical" level of normative reasoning, both moral codes and legal rules are subordinate to basic principles to which society is dedicated. These ethical principles establish what is meant by moral reason and serve as the criteria with reference to which laws are created and administered. They are also the basis of "ethical criticism" of legal standards that fail to respond to different conditions and values. In American law, for instance, commitment to equality entails uniformity and impartiality in legal requirements and in their application. In accordance with the principle of equal justice under the law, our judicial system limits the range of legal judgments to the specific "acts" of which the law takes cognizance. It also assures the right of appeal and submits its own decisions and the norms with which it operates to review.

The way laws are interpreted and enforced often provides insight into the basic commitments of a society. In many cases, however, they become static and are retained long after the circumstances and the values from which they originated have changed. Sometimes the requirements of the law are not merely irrelevant to important problems but are obstructive and harmful. Those laws which conflict with ethical norms or run counter to human needs and inclinations are frequently ignored, and decisions are made with reference to such principles as freedom, justice, least suffering, and the sanctity of life. Laws that persistently cause suffering or inequities are eventually challenged and revised on the basis of these values, which serve as our standards of ethical relevance and validity. This may take place within explicit legal reforms, but such innovations usually occur within an evolutionary course of judicial interpretation and accommodation.

The changing legal dimensions of suicide offer a good example of this process. For centuries, under English common law suicide was treated as a special crime and was punished severely. The victim's body was mutilated and given ignominious burial; his property was forfeited, and his family censured. In reaction to the severity of the law, incidents of suicide often were not reported as such, and gradually penal sanctions were modified and repealed. Such stringent penalties were never adopted by our legal system. Suicide is no longer against the law in most states of the United States. Twenty-three states have no penal statutes referring to suicide; eighteen states have no laws against this act but regard acts of aiding, advising, or encouraging another to commit suicide as a felony. Since it is usually not against the law to aid another in a noncriminal act, these acts are specified as crimes *sui generis;* nevertheless, prosecutions have been infrequent. Even in the nine states in which suicide attempts are felonies or misdemeanors, such laws are seldom enforced. During the past decade, the factors that have motivated this transition have also brought about a dramatic reversal of judicial precedent with regard to rewarding compensation in cases of suicidal death. This entire process reflects greater understanding of the causes and the consequences of suicide and concern for the needs of both the victims and their families. It suggests that, with the recognition that the problem often results from physical and emotional suffering, society is less interested in assessing guilt and enforcing punishment.

The important point to observe in connection with the problem of euthanasia is not simply that suicide, especially when it is committed in order to avoid suffering, might now be accepted or forgiven more easily. The primary issue is the way in which the law is shaped and applied in response to humane values and moral insight. From this perspective, the legal standards of medical practice can be understood, evaluated, and amended on the basis of the ethical principles from which they are derived, on the one hand, and in relation to the problems that arise in providing medical care, on the other.

THE MORAL AND LEGAL BASES
OF MEDICAL PRACTICE

One of the fundamental values underscored by our legal system is the sanctity of life. Implicit in the affirmation of this principle is a commitment to the inherent equality of all men, and because each individual is valued as an end in himself rather than as a means to social or political ends, his right to competent medical care is not contingent upon his position, wealth, or usefulness to society. Regard for man's physical and emotional integrity and respect for his autonomy are also involved in the recognition of human dignity. The rights that are implied by each of these values are ordered and protected by the moral and legal standards with reference to which medical decisions are made and judged.

1. The Value of Life

Because medical practice and law are motivated by the principle that life itself is intrinsically valuable, both work to prolong life and to protect it from injury and destruction. This orientation is clearly reflected in the sanctions of criminal law relative to homicide and is directly relevant to the question concerning the legitimacy of euthanasia. "Homicide" is a generic term that denotes the killing of a human being. As a legal concept, it refers to any act that causes or contributes materially to a person's death. In connection with the practice of medicine, it applies to any action or omission that precipitates a patient's death, even though he may be fatally ill and on the verge of death. The circumstances under which homicide is legally permitted or authorized indicate limitations imposed upon the principle

of the sanctity of life in relation to other values that shape
the law.

In Anglo-American law the difference between felonious
and nonfelonious homicide has been determined in the
course of a broad range of cases. Underlying this distinction
is the recognition that certain conditions alter or annul
moral responsibility and should be taken into account in
assessing criminal liability. Killing under such extenuating
circumstances is classified as either "justifiable" or "excusable" homicide. Following judicial precedents, penal codes
define the former as killing in self-defense, in defense of
family or property, or by necessity in the performance of a
legal duty. These actions are "justified" as expressions of
legitimate rights even though they have unfortunate consequences. Excusable homicide is interpreted as an accidental result of lawful conduct or self-defense in a sudden
affray, or homicide committed by someone who is not
legally competent.[4] As the term implies, legal "excuses"
exempt from liability those who are not necessarily without
fault, morally and legally, but whose actions or omissions are
either misdemeanors or fall outside the scope of law.
Decisions and laws differentiating noncriminal from criminal homicide reflect a clear priority of values on the basis of
which conflicting rights and responsibilities are ordered.

In common law, homicide for which there is no legal
justification or excuse is a felony. Performed with criminal
intent, deliberation, and premeditation, it constitutes murder, a first-degree felony.[5] Accordingly, the *Model Penal
Code* proposed by the American Law Institute defines
criminal homicide as murder when "(a) it is committed
purposely or knowingly; or (b) it is committed under
circumstances manifesting extreme indifference to the value
of human life."[6] In the absence of deliberation and
premeditation, unlawful killing is a second-degree felony. It
is often treated as voluntary manslaughter when death is

caused intentionally but as a spontaneous response to provocation,[7] and as involuntary manslaughter when death results unintentionally from negligence, reckless disregard for others, or illegal but nonfelonious acts.[8]

In some states, however, these concepts are interpreted differently in statutory law, and voluntary manslaughter is defined as a lesser degree of murder and involuntary manslaughter due to recklessness is referred to as "criminal negligence."[9] Depending upon the law within the jurisdiction in which the offense occurs, a physician may be held liable for either murder or voluntary manslaughter if he intentionally and deliberately takes his patient's life or fails to provide the necessary life-saving measures. He can be convicted of either involuntary manslaughter or criminal negligence if he unintentionally causes a patient's death through a gross lack of competence, because of carelessness or ignorance, or by an omission to fulfill an obligation imposed by law or contract.[10]

2. The Value of Health

The value of physical and psychological well-being is a corollary to the value of life. Consequently, our legal system enforces the level of competence that it requires of medical practice. Each member of society is expected to exercise "reasonable care" in order to avoid harming others. Failure to fulfill this obligation is often treated as "negligence," a term that is not necessarily synonymous with carelessness or inattendance.[11] As a legal concept, negligence comprehends unintentional malfeasance (an action that is illegal), misfeasance (an improper performance of lawful acts), and nonfeasance (an omission of legally prescribed behavior). It serves as the basis on which the law assesses civil and criminal liability when such actions or omissions constitute the proximate cause of injury or loss.

In connection with the practice of medicine, negligence is usually referred to as "malpractice," a more general concept which applies to misconduct on the part of the physician toward a patient.[12]

The standard of care which the doctor is required to meet is usually stated in broad terms in the law. Like most legal rules, however, it acquires specific meaning in the context of specific cases. Furthermore, it is a higher standard than is applied to other members of society. While the latter are expected to exercise the care of an "ordinary prudent man," the doctor is obligated to use special skills and knowledge. His judgment and conduct are evaluated in relation to the judgment and conduct of his colleagues, often in the same or in similar communities. The level of competence that the specialist must demonstrate is even higher than that expected of a general practitioner, for the decisions and actions of the latter are assessed on the basis of other specialists within his field.[13] The doctor's failure to meet this responsibility can lead to liability for the "damage" that his patient suffers.

Legal norms change as new methods and procedures are accepted by the medical profession, and the physician is expected to keep up to date in areas connected with his practice. Nevertheless, when scientific discoveries precipitate rapid innovations and new problems, the law tends to lag behind. Because its requirements are dependent upon a consensus within the medical community, it is seldom able to offer specific guidance for many of the difficult decisions having to do with the application of unprecedented techniques. There is, however, the general expectation that the doctor will prolong life as long as possible and will relieve suffering as effectively as possible. In most situations, this provides a basis for the physician to establish his legal responsibilities and to judge his conduct. Although these standards are usually sufficient, commitment to the values underlying these general requirements sometimes imposes incompatible demands. For exceptional yet not infrequent cases when the measures which extend life also prolong suffering, and those which relieve suffering curtail life, there are no generally accepted criteria for deciding the proper course. The same dilemma arises when the vital life processes of a hopeless, comatose patient are maintained at great suffering and expense for the patient's relatives.

3. The Value of Freedom

The principle of personal autonomy is of fundamental importance within our legal tradition. Insofar as the practice of medicine is concerned, the law operates to prescribe and enforce standards of conduct and to define and prohibit unacceptable behavior. In so doing, it provides the structure within which both the patient and the doctor are free, and it furnishes the instruments through which each can order his relationship to the other.[14] On the one hand, everyone is at liberty to accept or to refuse medical care; and, as pointed out in the A.M.A. "Principles of Medical Ethics," "a physician may choose whom he will serve." [15] On the other hand, however, when a patient seeks and obtains a doctor's service, the patient and the doctor enter into a contractual agreement that is legally binding as long as medical care is needed or, at least, the particular occasion for treatment persists, or until it is terminated by mutual consent, by the patient's dismissal, or by the physician's notice and withdrawal.[16] In the context of this relationship, their freedom is qualified not only by the limitations defined by law but also by their own self-imposed conditions.

On the basis of their voluntary contract, whether expressed or implied, rights are conferred and responsibilities are assumed which acquire legal significance. Any failure to fulfill these commitments or any refusal to abide by the terms of this transaction normally constitutes grounds for liability. By accepting a patient, the physician obligates himself to offer competent medical care in order to relieve suffering and to cure whenever possible. If he then abandons the patient—either by terminating his services without ample warning, by neglecting to provide "coverage" in an absence, or by refusing to respond to a call for help—or if he omits to provide the necessary treatment, his failure constitutes a breach of contract. Legal action in such cases closely parallels that of a civil suit for damages caused by the commission of a tort, and the doctor can be held responsible for the loss or suffering incurred by his lack of attention. If, however, the patient dies as a result of his negligence or omission, he may be held liable for criminal homicide. Whether he is charged with murder or manslaughter depends upon the circumstances of the case and the penal code of the state in which the death occurs.[17]

When a patient seeks medical attention, he expresses a willingness to permit an examination and a desire to receive the necessary care. By engaging a doctor's services and by entering a hospital, he too limits his own freedom and assumes the financial obligations involved in his treatment. In this process, however, the patient does not lose his autonomy or relinquish the right to make his own medical decisions. As Justice Benjamin N. Cardozo insisted in 1914, "every human being of adult years and sound mind has a right to determine what shall be done with his own body." [18] This principle is basic to our legal tradition and is not set aside by the contract between doctor and patient. In spite of its concern for life and physical well-being, common law guarantees this right and assures that whenever possible each person is given the freedom to reject beneficial and even life-saving treatment.[19]

The legal norms that reflect this value orientation are

quite explicit and require that the physician secure permission for all measures beyond the minor, routine procedures, such as blood tests and common medications, for which the "implied consent" of the doctor-patient relationship is clearly sufficient. When the patient is legally competent, the law usually gives priority to his decision; otherwise, it often holds the closest relative or a guardian responsible for deciding in his behalf. Not only must the physician acquire permission to act, but he must stay within the limits of the authority that he is granted. Even though this limitation may seem unnecessarily confining and counter to his own medical opinion, he seldom may render medical or surgical treatment that is different from, or more extensive than, that to which the patient has given consent. Obviously, the patient is not expected to be more intelligent or to exercise better medical judgment than the doctor, but as Prof. Dan B. Dobbs has pointed out, "it is not physical health that is being protected but his right to decide his own destiny." [20]

Although this principle is well established, the charges that may be brought against a physician who fails to obtain or to stay within the limits of consent depend largely on the theory of liability that has been affirmed in the jurisdiction in which the incident occurs. In most cases, such conduct leads only to civil liability, but some courts consider it technical assault and battery, which might, under local laws, lead to criminal liability as well.[21] *Mohr* v. *Williams* (1905)[22] seems to have been the first instance in which tort liability was imposed on a doctor for going beyond his patient's consent, and this decision was followed in *Pratt* v. *Davis* (1906)[23] and in *Schloendorff* v. *Society of New York Hospital* (1914).[24] In cases based on this approach, the patient must show only that the doctor acted without permission. He is not required to prove proximate cause or to provide expert medical witnesses, which are usually necessary in a malpractice suit. Since the issue in question is the absence of legal consent, the fact that the treatment was beneficial or skilled does not constitute a defense.

Even prior to *Mohr*, common law acknowledged the patient's right to make his own medical decisions. In cases involving unauthorized treatment, it interpreted the doctor's conduct as a violation of the responsibilities implicit within the doctor-patient relationship. Consequently, his failure to secure or to comply with a patient's consent was regarded as negligence rather than as assault and battery. Courts in a number of subsequent cases have followed this reasoning and have allowed patients to sue for malpractice, especially when the statute of limitations would have ruled out an action based on tort liability. In so doing, they have preserved this as an alternate course of action. In some states, the "contract of employment" between doctor and patient has become the primary factor governing the theory of liability under which a physician can be charged for having acted without proper authority.[25] Within either approach, however, the issue is the patient's autonomy.

Consistent with its affirmation of this principle, the law also recognizes the patient's right to the information necessary so that his freedom and his decision may have meaning. It therefore regards uninformed consent, whether general or specific, express or implied, as having no legal significance, and holds the physician responsible to provide the patient appropriate instructions, warnings, and alternatives. In the course of interpreting this obligation in relation to different circumstances, courts have required that he disclose all reasonable and recognized results, inevitable results, probable results, and possible results.[26] At the same time, the law permits and expects the doctor to exercise prudence in fulfilling this responsibility. In *Salgo* v. *Leland Stanford Jr. University Board of Trustees*, for example, the California court acknowledged that, in view of the importance of the patient's mental and emotional condition, "the physician has such discretion consistent, of course, with the full disclosure of facts necessary to an informed consent." [27] It also established one of the most exacting standards concerning the extent to which a patient must be informed. In this case, which involved a relatively new and dangerous procedure from which the patient suffered permanent paralysis, the court ruled that the physician may not withhold "*any* facts which are necessary to form the basis of an intelligent consent by the patient to the proposed treatment, likewise the physician may not minimize the known dangers of a procedure in order to induce his patient's consent." [28]

Although this decision is frequently cited for the principle that consent must be informed in order to be valid, the standards that have been applied in many cases are far less stringent. A North Carolina court, for example, has stated that "a surgeon, except in emergency, should make a reasonable disclosure of the risk involved . . . if the operation involves a known risk." [29] It concluded, however, that his obligation depends on the nature of the risk and whether a reasonable man in his position and with his knowledge of the patient would conclude that, if informed, he would not withdraw consent. In other states, the law requires that the physician inform the patient only when and to the extent to which other responsible practitioners in the same community and under the same or in similar circumstances would disclose the risks or consequences of the proposed treatment.[30]

Many doctors prefer the last approach, because it gives them much greater latitude to determine the instructions necessary for informed consent in a broad range of cases. When this standard is applied, the patient must not only prove that there was a breach of duty but must also produce expert medical testimony in order to show that the physician had a responsibility to offer the information in question.

When this procedure is followed, the patient's right to determine what shall be done with his own body depends upon the integrity and the prevailing customs of the medical community. This kind of consensus with regard to "reasonable care" provides a necessary basis for establishing and protecting the patient's basic rights to competent medical treatment. Nevertheless, his rights to consent should have priority over the dictates of "customary procedures."

Insofar as the law is concerned, the doctor's right and duty to render medical care are contingent upon the patient's informed consent. Nevertheless, there are important exceptions to this general rule when the patient is unable to exercise his prerogative. Some courts have held that the physician is then at liberty to provide emergency aid and have suggested that "consent on the part of the injured person would be implied." [31] Other courts, however, have concluded that he is obligated, rather than privileged, to act in an emergency. In *Pratt*, for example, the Illinois court advised that "in such event, the surgeon may lawfully, and it is his duty to, perform such operation as good surgery demands, without consent." [32] This opinion was affirmed in *Jackovach* v. *Yocum*, one of the leading decisions on this requirement. In this case, the Iowa court held that "if a surgeon is confronted with an emergency which endangers the life or the health of the patient, it is his duty to do what the occasion demands with the usual and the customary practice among physicians and surgeons in the same or similar localities, without the consent of the patient." [33] The concepts "right" and "liberty" are more appropriate to use in describing the doctor's legal responsibilities in emergencies that arise outside an established doctor-patient relationship. The concept "duty" is more accurate to define his obligations on the basis of this contract. In either case, the law makes it possible for the doctor to render life-saving treatment for the sake of lives that might be lost if he were required to act at his own peril.

Even though it assumes that most persons would request emergency care, the law continues to give priority to the autonomy of each patient when this assumption is in question. Consequently, when accused of having violated a patient's right to be "let alone," the physician must show not only that an emergency existed that threatened the former's life or health, but also that the patient was unable to consent, that a reasonable man would have permitted the treatment, and that there was no reason to believe that this particular patient would have done otherwise.[34] Obviously there are occasions, especially when a patient is confused, delirious, or insane, in which the doctor must ignore his refusal to consent. The most difficult moral and legal problems arise when the physician's responsibility to prolong life comes into direct conflict with his obligation to acknowledge the patient's right to refuse life-saving measures. Called upon to resolve this dilemma when patients have refused blood transfusions because of their religious beliefs, the courts have rendered *ad hoc* decisions in the light of the competing claims and values in each case. Some have permitted and others have refused to permit the doctor to act, but no precedent has been established altering the basic legal principle that each person is the master of his own body.

LEGAL NORMS RELATIVE TO EUTHANASIA

Laws are part and parcel of an entire system of moral norms with reference to which decisions are made and actions are evaluated. They are created and amended in accordance with the same ethical values to which society is committed. Nevertheless, there are important differences in the interpretations of basic normative concepts and between moral and legal judgments. Furthermore, in some cases there are serious inconsistencies between legal principles and judicial decisions, the law in theory and the law in practice. These factors must be taken into account in order to comprehend the legal dimensions of the practice of euthanasia and in order to shape and apply legal norms that are relevant to human needs and to the realities of terminal medical care.

1. Homicide: Murder and Euthanasia

The terms "murder" and "euthanasia" have quite different connotations as moral and as legal concepts. The basic source of this discrepancy lies in the difference between a general (moral) and a technical (legal) definition of "murder" as homicide committed with *malice aforethought* and without legal justification or excuse. In most cases, the failure to understand the legal denotations of the terms "malice" and "malice aforethought" causes little difficulty. When, for example, a deliberate and unlawful homicide occurs because of anger or hatred, moral and legal judgments often coincide, at least in identifying the offense as murder. Sharply conflicting opinions are expressed, however, when life is taken for reasons that are generally considered humane rather than malicious. These are indicative of a significant difference between a moral and a strictly legal perspective.

From a moral point of view, motive is usually one of the most important considerations in the evaluation of human behavior, and malice is thought of as a malevolent motivation. From a precise legal viewpoint, motive has far less significance and is not regarded as a necessary component of any crime. In common law and statutory definitions of felonious homicide, "malice" is equivalent to "intent" and serves to differentiate murder, or intentional homicide, from

LETTER OF THE LAW AND SPIRIT OF MERCY 143

manslaughter, or unintentional homicide.[35] Evidence concerning motive is admitted in some cases in order to
demonstrate the defendant's inability to entertain criminal
intent[36] or to demonstrate that his action was in self-
defense.[37] Otherwise, it is irrelevant as a defense to the
crime. Such evidence is permitted, however, in support of
the prosecution's proof of the defendant's intent, but this is
not required for conviction.[38]

As the term implies, mercy killing is performed for the
sake of one who is suffering in order to secure relief and an
easy, dignified death. Motive is the crucial issue that
distinguishes this act from "murder" in moral discourse.
Unlike homicide committed from malice, mercy killing is
often considered a humane and a justifiable, or at least
excusable, response on the part of those who are responsible
for caring for the dying. In criminal law, however, "humanitarian" motives are not recognized as a legitimate "justification" or "excuse" for homicide,[39] and "malice" comprehends "not only anger, and revenge, but every other
unlawful and unjustifiable motive." [40] Since mercy is not
differentiated from malice, in the absence of mitigating
circumstances, there is no legal basis for distinguishing
euthanasia from murder.

2. "Voluntary" and "Involuntary" Euthanasia

The terms "voluntary" and "involuntary" with reference
to euthanasia do not have the same implications as moral
and as legal concepts. The problem of deciding who should
determine the course to follow in providing terminal care is
one of the most difficult moral questions posed by the
presence of suffering and by the life-saving innovations
within medical science. Both in response to cases in which
mercy killing is performed and in the arguments favoring its
practice, a basic distinction is usually made between taking

life in accordance with the patient's desire, on the one hand, and causing death without or against his consent, on the other. Voluntary euthanasia is often considered much less reprehensible than involuntary euthanasia and is sometimes thought of as warranted, especially when suffering is intense or prolonged and there is no hope of a reasonable recovery. Although this orientation may be justifiable on the basis of the value of personal autonomy, it is frequently somewhat unrealistic in view of the problem of securing *informed* consent under the conditions in which terminal decisions must be rendered. When the patient is emotionally disturbed, under sedation, unconscious, or otherwise incompetent to decide for himself, the choice must be made for him, and on the basis of his "presumed" desire, between prolonging life, passive euthanasia, and active euthanasia.

Under Anglo-American jurisprudence, the victim's consent is not recognized as a legitimate defense to criminal homicide. In one of the leading cases for this principle, a Tennessee court held that:

> Murder is no less murder because the homicide is committed at the desire of the victim. He who kills another upon his desire and command is, in the judgment of the law, as much a murderer as if he had done it merely of his own head.[41]

Assisting someone to commit suicide is closely related to homicide upon request and is often treated as a criminal offense, even where suicide is not considered a crime. In *State* v. *Roberts,* a Michigan case that is frequently cited to this effect, the defendant was found guilty of murder for having prepared the poison with which his wife, who was incurably afflicted with multiple sclerosis, committed suicide.[42] An appeal was based on the fact that suicide was not a crime in Michigan, but the conviction for murder by means of poison was sustained. Since it is usually not a felony to aid another to perform a noncriminal act, some states, as noted above, define aiding and abetting suicide as a crime *sui generis*. New York, for example, interprets such acts as either manslaughter in the first degree or as a less serious felony, depending upon whether or not the attempt was successful.

The way in which homicide upon request or consent and accessories to suicide are dealt with in the common law tradition is indicative of a basic commitment to life as sacred and inalienable. A person's freedom to refuse life-saving treatment is among the few exceptions to this principle that are legally sanctioned. As a rule the law gives priority to the value of life and denies the right to choose between life and death. Consequently, when it differentiates between voluntary and involuntary homicide, it is concerned with the "intention" of the actor rather than with the consent or request of his victim. A physician who unintentionally causes a patient's death through negligence, inattention, or culpable ignorance may be held liable for involuntary manslaughter, regardless of the patient's desire to die.[43] In most cases in which a person is killed in order to relieve suffering, whether at his request or without his consent, the act is intentional, and it is usually performed with premeditation and deliberation. Since the law does not take into account the actor's motives and does not acknowledge the victim's right to choose to die, both voluntary and involuntary euthanasia are equivalent to murder or, at least, voluntary manslaughter.[44]

3. "Active" and "Passive" Euthanasia

Similarly, "active" and "passive" euthanasia have differing implications in legal and in moral discourse. They serve, however, to distinguish between "acts" and "omissions" that cause death and are important because of a basic moral distinction between killing and failing to take affirmative action to save. With few exceptions, when they are deliberate both are regarded as immoral because of the value of human life; but terminating a person's life is usually understood to be more serious than merely allowing him to die. The way in which this difference is interpreted and expressed in legal standards does not always correspond with the prevailing moral judgments.

Many who disappove of taking life also oppose the practice of prolonging life when recovery is impossible and such efforts extend or contribute to the patient's suffering. They often consider his personal autonomy to be of greater value than his life *per se* and regard death as preferable to the loss of dignity from desperate attempts to maintain a painful or an unconscious existence. Consequently, even though "acts" that terminate life are judged to be immoral, "omissions" either by failing to apply or by withdrawing life-sustaining measures are sometimes thought of as necessary and morally responsible. In the course of providing terminal care, however, it is frequently difficult to distinguish between morally acceptable "omissions" and unacceptable "actions."

This distinction between passive and active euthanasia is especially ambiguous when life is prolonged by means of respirators, heart-lung machines, and other devices that might be "turned off" to allow a patient to die. On the one hand, if it differentiates between what is acceptable and unacceptable solely on the basis of a distinction between inaction and overt action, terminating supportive measures must be interpreted as active euthanasia. If, once they are introduced, these procedures cannot be "turned off," decisions to employ them require medical foresight that is usually impossible in order to avoid tragic consequences in terms of physical and emotional suffering. On the other hand, if this distinction is based on the difference between "causing death" and "permitting death," the removal of necessary supportive devices can be understood quite differently. Dr. George P. Fletcher, an assistant professor of law at the University of Washington, suggests that the perspective from which we tend to identify respirators as an artificial means of prolonging life when a patient is on the verge of death allows us to interpret their discontinuation as a means of permitting death. "Because we are prompted to refer to the activity of turning off respirators as an activity permitting death to occur, rather than causing death," he argues, "we may classify the case as an omission rather than as an act." [45] This approach makes the distinction between active and passive euthanasia contingent not only upon the patient's condition but also upon the time and place in which it is made, for the difference between the "natural" and the "artificial" is relative to constantly changing standards of medical practice.

These factors are frequently taken into account in medical decisions and in moral and legal judgments, but such considerations are not reflected in the legal norms that are applicable to terminal decisions. Just as a patient's suffering or his desire to die is not accepted as a legitimate defense for criminal homicide, the fact that he is dying is not recognized as a justification or an excuse for homicide under common law. Furthermore, there is no legal equivalent to the moral distinction between "causing" and "permitting" a patient to die, which serves to permit a doctor to bring about death by withholding or by terminating life-preserving measures. Even when he interrupts treatment or administers a potentially lethal narcotic solely for the purpose of relieving suffering, if he recognizes that death is substantially likely to follow, he is said to "intend" the consequences of his actions.[46] Although the law does not impose a general affirmative duty to render emergency assistance to save life, the contractual relationship between doctor and patient establishes this obligation. Conse-

quently, the difference between active and passive euthanasia has little significance insofar as laws governing medical
practice are concerned. Except when a patient, by refusing
to consent to necessary treatment, relieves the doctor of his
legal duty to protect life, the doctor's failure to fulfill this
responsibility is equivalent to an affirmative act. Furthermore, in the absence of mitigating circumstances, his
intentional action or omission in order to terminate a
patient's life is a first-degree felony, unless liability for fatal
omissions is reduced by statutory law.[47]

In the last analysis, it should be observed that this
summary of legal standards relative to euthanasia is a
statement of the law in theory only. The different ways in
which basic normative concepts are interpreted and applied
in moral and in legal discourse result in misunderstandings
and conflicting decisions. Furthermore, they give rise to
inconsistent standards for terminal medical practice and
render already complex problems even more difficult.
Nevertheless, careful attention to these sources of difficulty
and consistent moral and legal reasoning can provide a basis
on which to interpret and to "correct" the legal norms in
relation to fundamental ethical principles and moral norms.

LEGAL PRACTICE RELATIVE TO EUTHANASIA

Law includes not only statutes and precedents, which
define rights and prescribe responsibilities, but also a
process of administration in which legal norms and sanctions are applied. In the selection and interpretation of laws
relevant to particular cases and in the evaluation of
appropriate punitive measures, a certain amount of judicial
discretion is required in order to approximate justice, the
criterion with reference to which specific standards and the
entire legal system are evaluated. As a rule, laws that have

become obsolete are "corrected" in this process, and those which would make harsh demands, if they were applied inflexibly, are tempered in relation to the circumstances of specific cases. Consequently, a thorough understanding of the law requires an examination of the way it operates.

1. Failure to Indict

In relation to the problem of euthanasia, there are serious discrepancies between the law in theory and the law in action. Although the practice of euthanasia is a felony as a matter of legal principle, prosecutors and grand juries tend not to indict those who kill in order to relieve suffering or to prevent a prolonged unconscious existence when there is no hope of recovery. In a case that occurred in 1938, for example, a grand jury in Nassau County, New York, refused to indict Harry C. Johnson. He admitted to having asphyxiated his wife because she was suffering with incurable cancer and wanted to die. Because such decisions are usually made "off the record," or at least without attracting public attention, it is impossible to determine how frequently they occur.

The law also tends to overlook the practice of passive euthanasia altogether. Because of advances in medical science, doctors must often choose to terminate life-preserving measures or omit to perform routine emergency treatment in order to permit hopeless patients to die. Theoretically, they are as legally obligated to prolong the lives of the suffering and dying as they are to save the lives of those for whom recovery is possible. In either case they are liable for failing to act to avert death, but doctors are seldom charged for failing to prolong the life of terminal patients. This may be due primarily to the inherent problem of obtaining a conviction because of the difficulty of proving causation and because of the humane response of juries in such cases.

However, it may reflect a tacit approval of passive euthanasia on the part of those who administer the law.

2. Failure to Convict

Even when cases involving active euthanasia are prosecuted, convictions are rare, and one can find no record of a case to support the theory of liability for passive euthanasia. Apparently, neither doctors nor laymen have been found guilty of having allowed patients to die in order to end their suffering. Furthermore, jurors are reluctant to convict those accused of murder or manslaughter for having taken life out of mercy for the radically deformed, the imbecile, and the dying. In State v. Greenfield (New York, 1939), for example, Louis Greenfield was charged with first-degree manslaughter in the death of his seventeen-year-old son, Jerry, who was said to have been an "incurable imbecile" with a mentality of a two-year-old. Prior to the indictment, District Attorney Samuel J. Foeley admitted that he was hesitant to prosecute such "a sad case." In the course of the trial, Greenfield confessed that he chloroformed his son because he "loved him, and it was the will of God." He claimed that his action was directed by an "unseen hand" and an "unknown voice." A sympathetic jury found him not guilty.

Although the question of euthanasia is clearly a primary issue in such cases, acquittals are usually based on an acceptable defense, such as temporary insanity, rather than on such defenses as "humanitarian motive" or "homicide at the request or consent of the victim." In State v. Braunsdorf (Michigan, 1950), the defendant, Eugene Braunsdorf, was judged not guilty by reason of temporary insanity for having shot his spastic-crippled, twenty-nine-year-old daughter, Virginia. In State v. Paight (Connecticut, 1950), Carol Paight was charged with manslaughter for having shot her father after an exploratory operation revealed that he had cancer of the stomach. Her defense claimed a "cancer phobia" as a result of the death of two aunts, and she was acquitted on the basis of temporary insanity. In *State* v. *Zygmaniak* (New Jersey, 1973), Lester Zygmaniak was charged with first-degree murder in the slaying of his brother, George. The incident occurred in the Jersey Shore Medical Center after his brother had been paralyzed in a motorcycle accident. Lester testified that he had shot his brother at his request in order to end his suffering. The defense, however, was based on temporary insanity. Although one psychiatrist claimed that he was sane, two other psychiatrists testified that he was deranged at the time of the shooting, and Lester was acquitted.

In *State* v. *Sander* (New Hampshire, 1950), Dr. Herman N. Sander was found innocent of the charge of murder in the death of a terminal cancer patient, Mrs. Abbie Borrato, on the ground that the prosecution had failed to prove the *corpus delicti*. At the time of her death, the defendant noted on her medical chart that he had administered "ten cc. of air intravenously repeated four times" and that she had "expired within ten minutes after this started." He later dictated this to his nurse and gave the same information to local law enforcement authorities before and after his arrest. At the trial, the attending nurse testified that the patient was still "gasping" when Dr. Sander injected the air, but he argued that she was already dead when he acted and that his entry on her record was only "a casual dictation . . . merely a way of closing out the chart." His defense counsel explicitly denied that euthanasia was a defense or an issue in the case, and a pathologist was called on to testify as an expert witness that Mrs. Borrato's death was caused by factors other than the injection of air. His defense was based on the prosecution's failure to prove beyond a reasonable doubt that the defendant had any motive or intent to kill her, that he injected a lethal dose, that the needle actually reached a vein, that the vein was "open" to the heart, that embolus was formed, that air embolism was the cause of death, or that the patient was even alive at the time of the injection. The evidence that was cited against Dr. Sander by the prosecution included his entry in the hospital record and his pre-trial confessions. The jury ruled in favor of the defense that no causal relation had been established between his acts and his patient's death.

State v. *Montemarano* (New York, 1973) is the only other case of alleged mercy killing in which a medical doctor has been tried for murder. Dr. Vincent A. Montemarano was the chief surgical resident of the Nassau County Medical Center. In December, 1972, he administered a lethal dose of potassium chloride to Eugene Bauer, a fifty-nine-year-old patient with throat cancer. Bauer was comatose and was said to have only two days to live. As in the Sander case, the injection was witnessed by a nurse and recorded in the medical records. Dr. Montemarano claimed that the drug, which is sometimes used to retard cancer, was not given in order to kill the patient. As in the previous case, also, the jury returned a verdict of not guilty.

In the case of *People* v. *Werner* (Illinois, 1958), the court followed a quite different procedure in order to spare the defendant, Otto Werner, "the stigma of a finding of guilty." Werner was arraigned on a charge of murder for having suffocated his wife, Anna, who was bedridden and suffering from advanced rheumatoid arthritis. In accordance with an agreement between the defense and prosecuting attorneys, he was permitted to enter a plea of guilty to the crime of manslaughter. The court ruled on this plea finding the defendant guilty and heard an application on his behalf for probation. In response to the evidence from the deceased's physician concerning her condition and suffering and the testimony of his children and minister with regard to his love and attention for her, the court allowed Werner to withdraw his plea of guilty and entertained a plea of not guilty. In explaining this decision, Chief Justice A. L. Marovitz observed that "if he were tried with a jury, and testimony was brought out of this devotion and care to his wife in her incurable illness and of her constant pain and suffering, the jury would not be inclined to return a verdict of guilty." [48] Accordingly, he found the defendant innocent.

3. Lenient Sentences and Probation

Although prosecutors are hesitant to indict and juries are disinclined to convict on evidence of euthanasia, there have been convictions for homicides that seem to have been committed in order to relieve suffering. With few exceptions, however, the potentially harsh consequences of a guilty verdict have been avoided. This is sometimes accomplished by a conviction for a less serious crime than warranted by the evidence. In one such case in 1941, Louis Repouille was indicted for manslaughter in the first degree for having chloroformed his thirteen-year-old son, a hopeless idiot, who was radically deformed, mute, blind, and incontinent. To the four other children dependent upon him for their support, Repouille was a responsible parent, and a compassionate jury returned a verdict of manslaughter in the second degree with a recommendation of "utmost clemency." The court imposed a five- to ten-year sentence but stayed its execution and placed him on probation, from which he was discharged five years later.

In the meantime, Repouille applied to become a naturalized citizen, but his petition was dismissed because of a statutory requirement that one must demonstrate "good moral character" within the five years preceding an application for citizenship. In rejecting his request, however,

Justice Learned Hand questioned whether his crime did in fact violate generally accepted moral standards and virtually invited him to reapply. Justice Hand pointed out that:

> It is reasonably clear that the jury which tried Repouille did not feel any moral repulsion at his crime. Although it was inescapably murder in the first degree, not only did they bring in a verdict that was flatly in the face of facts and utterly absurd—for manslaughter in the second degree presupposes that the killing has not been deliberate—but they coupled even that with a recommendation which showed in substance they wished to exculpate the offender. Moreover, it is also plain, from the sentence which he imposed, that the judge could not have seriously disagreed with their recommendation.[49]

In other cases, those who have killed out of mercy have been convicted as charged but have received relatively lenient sentences. Harold A. Mohr, for example, was found guilty of voluntary manslaughter in 1950 for having shot a brother who was blind and suffering from cancer. Although the latter apparently had requested to die, two other brothers testified for the state against Mohr. The jury, however, recommended mercy, and the court imposed a sentence of from three to six years in prison and a fine of five hundred dollars. In so doing, the judge explained that Mohr had acted as a martyr and must suffer punishment as the price of martyrdom.

Even when strict sentences are handed down, other avenues remain open by which they can be tempered. In a Massachusetts case in 1944, John F. Noxon was convicted of first-degree murder and was sentenced to death for having electrocuted his six-month-old mongoloid son. Although there was evidence to indicate that he had wrapped his son with an electric cord and had placed him in wet diapers on a silver tray, Noxon claimed that death was accidental. This defense may have been one of the primary reasons for his conviction or, at least, for the death sentence. As Prof. Yale Kamisar has observed, "a full presentation of the appealing 'mercy-killing' circumstances would be more difficult under the theory Noxon adopted than under the typical 'temporary insanity' defense." [50] Nevertheless, due to "extenuating circumstances" which he did not explain, Gov. M. J. Tobin commuted his sentence to life imprisonment in 1946. There may be some doubt concerning Tobin's claim that "mercy-killing, so-called" could not be regarded as an extenuating circumstance and that it was not a factor in his decision. Two years later Noxon's sentence was further commuted to from six years to life in order to make parole possible, and shortly thereafter he was paroled.

ALTERNATIVES FOR DEALING WITH EUTHANASIA

The most obvious inference that can be drawn from cases involving euthanasia is that the law in practice does not correspond with strictly legal principles. The law in theory is a product of medical ethics and social norms that take seriously the role of the physician as the preserver of life. Accordingly, it underscores the expectation that life be preserved as a legal responsibility, but it does not reflect the ambiguities and conflicts that arise when other medical and social values are incompatible with this requirement. Such inconsistencies are expressed, however, in the compromises of the law and of professional medical ethics in the context of specific cases. In both legal and medical practice there is a point at which the conflict between the obligation to preserve life and the toll taken by it on the patient and the family is recognized and taken into account. The decisions that are made and the judgments that are rendered in these

cases suggest that we tend to regard the practice of
euthanasia less as a moral evil or crime and more as the
unfortunate but necessary and humane response to human
need and suffering.

1. Administrative and Judicial Discretion

The problem posed by the tacit acceptance of euthanasia
is that of translating it into legal standards and practices in a
way that is consistent with the values underlying our moral
and legal traditions. Some, arguing against changes in the
law, hold that there are limits to what can be provided by a
legal structure. They point out that, although compromises
with the usual severity of the law are sometimes necessary,
"hard cases make bad laws." They warn that the inviolability of human life, which is preserved by the law, would be
undermined if the practice of euthanasia were legalized.
They conclude that even though in extreme cases it might
have to be set aside, this principle should be protected even
if other values must be sacrificed.

Harry Kalven, for example, is concerned with the "unwanted repercussions on the delicate forces which restrain
killing" that an official approval of euthanasia might have.
He fears that "perhaps any endorsement by society here
will be read by some as a general approval of suicide and a
general ratification of crime done for a benevolent motive."
Because of the difficulty of establishing safeguards to secure
equitable treatment and, at the same time, to prevent abuse,
Kalven favors "leaving things as they are and trusting for
awhile yet to the imperfect but elastic equity in the
administration of the law as written." [51]

Yale Kamisar also admits that the existing law on
euthanasia is hardly perfect, but he insists that "if it is not
too good, neither . . . is it much worse than the rest of the
criminal law." [52] Against proposed legislative changes to

legalize euthanasia, Kamisar warns of the danger of mistakes. He argues that unless the need for authorized conduct is compelling enough to override this danger, the threat of mistakes is a conclusive reason against such authorization. Although he concedes that "in a narrow sense" it is evil for a terminal and suffering patient to have to suffer even if only for a little while, Kamisar concludes that we can justify their prolonged suffering in the same way that we justify imprisonment or death by the state, that is, for "social interests." [53]

2. Bills to Permit Euthanasia

Underlying the arguments in favor of legalizing euthanasia, there is a commitment to the principles of least suffering and individual autonomy. These values are affirmed over the principle of the inviolability of life, at least in terminal cases. Those who recommend changing the law in order to avoid the negative consequences of legal compromise argue that "bad laws make hard cases." In the first place, they point out that special *ad hoc* judgments do not establish legal precedents with reference to which terminal medical decisions can be made and evaluated. In the second place, they underscore the inequities that result from legal and extralegal maneuvers in the administration of the law. They insist that each person should have the right to die with dignity but only those for whom a doctor is willing to act at his own peril are permitted to exercise this right. Furthermore, they warn that the fact that the law has been lenient in other cases is no guarantee that a doctor would not be indicted, tried, and prosecuted for practicing euthanasia. In the third place, those who advocate legal reforms claim that the failure to apply existing laws in some cases and the leniency with which they are applied in others undermines public confidence in the law. According to Helen Silving, the use of legal technicalities to correct inequities in the law tends to give the impression that the law is "a magic formula rather than an honest tool of meting out justice." [54]

Suggestions for legal changes to permit euthanasia range from proposals that would authorize the state to sponsor its practice to directions for exempting the medical profession from liability for mercy killing in terminal cases. In a bill introduced in the House of Commons in 1936, the Voluntary Euthanasia Legislation Society attempted to legalize voluntary active euthanasia. In order to overcome the fear that such a measure would be open to abuse, it recommended elaborate safeguards and restricted eligibility to patients over twenty-one years of age who suffer from an incurable and fatal disease involving severe pain. Those who qualified were to be granted or denied euthanasia through the following procedure:

a. They were to be required to make application on specially prepared forms in the presence of at least two witnesses.

b. Completed applications and two medical certificates, one by the attending physician and one by another qualified physician, would be sent to a Euthanasia Referee appointed by the Minister of Health.

c. Before granting permission for euthanasia, this referee was to satisfy himself, by a personal interview and otherwise, that the requisite conditions have been fulfilled and that the patient fully understands the nature and purpose of the application.

d. If a permit were granted, there was to be a lapse of seven days before it became "operative." In the meantime, the nearest relative was to be informed and allowed to appeal to a Court of Summary

        Jurisdiction if one or more of the necessary conditions had not been met.

e. If the permit were not canceled within this period, euthanasia was to be granted in the presence of an official witness by the doctor specified by the permit.

Under this plan, the responsibility for controlling the practice of euthanasia was to be assigned to the Minister of Health. He was to have the authority to make regulations for licensing doctors to practice euthanasia, for assigning the duties and fees of euthanasia referees, and for prescribing the procedures and forms to be used.

This bill served as the model for the program sponsored by the Euthanasia Society of America. Its Proposed Bill to Legalize Euthanasia, which was introduced in the New York State legislature in 1938 and 1947, was designed to permit the practice of euthanasia for patients over twenty-one who suffer "from severe physical pain caused by a disease for which no remedy affording relief or recovery is at the time known to medical science." [55] The basic differences between the American and British bills were procedural. According to the provisions of the former, jurisdiction to grant euthanasia would have been assigned to "any justice of the Supreme Court of the judicial district, in which the patient resides or may be, or any judge of a county court of any county in which the patient resides or may be." [56] The proposed process through which one could secure legally sanctioned euthanasia was as follows:

a. A petition is completed by the patient and signed by two witnesses.
b. This application and a form signed by the attending physician is filed with a court of appropriate jurisdiction.
c. The court appoints a "committee of three compe-

tent persons, who are not opposed to euthanasia . . . , of whom at least two must be physicians." They are directed to examine the patient and the doctor in order to determine whether or not the patient understands the purpose of his petition and qualifies under the provisions of the law.

d. If the committee's finding is affirmative, the court grants the petition within three days, "unless there is reason to believe that the report is erroneous or untrue."

e. Euthanasia is then administered "in the presence of the committee, or any two members thereof, . . . by a person chosen by the patient or by said committee, or any two members thereof, with the patient's consent."

f. If the petition is denied, the court is required to state its reason in writing. The patient is allowed to make an appeal "to the appellate division of the supreme court, and/or to the Court of Appeals." [57]

This plan and the measures sponsored by the Euthanasia Society in England were subjected to essentially the same criticism. On the one hand, their restrictions and formalities, which were designed to prevent abuse, were said to be out of keeping with the very idea of mercy and inappropriate in the presence of suffering and dying patients. On the other hand, these limits were said to be too narrow to meet the problems for which the bill was intended, and the elaborate precautions were criticized as inadequate to rule out error and misuse of legalized euthanasia.

In response to the charge that such measures would contribute to the anxiety and distress of dying patients, Glanville Williams has recommended that "reformers might be well advised, in their next proposal, to abandon all their cumbrous safeguards . . . giving the medical practitioner a wide discretion and trusting in his good sense." [58] He suggests that such a bill should include provisions that would permit a physician to increase pain-relieving drugs as a patient's need grew. It should permit him to refrain from taking steps to prolong the life of a dying patient in order to save him from severe pain. Finally, it should enable him, after consultation with another physician, to accelerate the death of a terminal patient who requests to die.[59]

According to Professor Williams, these measures would leave the practice of mercy killing entirely to the discretion and the conscience of the physician and would make it a part of ordinary medical practice. Thus, it would free him from fear of the law and enable him to concentrate solely on the needs of his patients. This proposal calling for the unrestricted authorization of both active and passive voluntary euthanasia is much more permissive than previous bills. His proposal is open to the same criticism that has been leveled against the latter. The basic objection, as expressed by Professor Kamisar, is that it "raises too great a risk of abuse and mistake to warrant a change in the existing law." [60]

Williams, however, sought to provide the safeguards of consent without the formality of earlier euthanasia bills. This basic principle of his legislative suggestion is found in bills recently introduced in a number of states. A Florida bill, for example, would permit a request to be made by any competent person who is at least eighteen and whose condition has been declared by two physicians to be terminal. Two Wisconsin bills would allow the formal request to be made in advance of an illness, and one of the bills would provide for the request to be made on behalf of a minor or an incompetent adult. Steps are specified in each bill to permit the patient to revoke his request easily. Physicians acting in accordance with these bills would be guaranteed freedom from civil and criminal liability.

Such bills to permit a patient to request to die with dignity are much more conservative than previous proposals to legalize euthanasia. Bills in Florida, Oregon, West Virginia, and Wisconsin would only sanction the right to refuse artificial, extraordinary, or heroic measures to prolong life. Bills in Idaho and Montana would go a little farther by permitting active measures to cause death, such as turning off life-sustaining equipment. If passed, these bills would only serve to provide legal sanctions for practices that are already common in terminal medical care. This is especially interesting to note in view of the fact that no state has yet enacted specific legislation to sanction such practices. In the final analysis, however, patients already have the legal right to refuse treatment to prolong life.

3. Measures to Mitigate Punishment

Rather than completely exempting euthanasia from penal law by legalizing its practice within narrow and clearly defined limits, Helen Silving prefers a method of reducing the penalty of homicide when it is motivated by mercy. She believes that this would best be accomplished through a thoroughgoing reform of the law in order to create a "system" of criminal law instead of a loose collection of incoherent criminal provisions. In such a system, closely related unlawful acts should be conceived of as a class rather than as isolated crimes, and motive, rather than premeditation and deliberation, should be regarded as a substantive element differentiating between the degrees within each class. As examples of this approach to criminal law, Silving cites modern continental European penal codes, especially those of Germany, Switzerland, and Norway, that define, classify, and punish criminal behavior not according to "types" of criminal acts but with reference to the guilt of the actor as indicated by his motivation and the manner of his performance.[61] In support of her argument for revising American codes on these models, she points to the "circumvention of legal provisions, lack of uniformity of adjudication, and public dissatisfaction" in euthanasia cases in this country and in England.

Two "legislative techniques" are suggested for distinguishing between homicide cases on the basis of motive. On the one hand, courts could be granted broad discretion to classify cases within the various types of homicide and to mete out punishment in accordance with the motive involved. On the other hand, the statutes of a comprehensive penal code might enumerate particularly reprehensible motives or motives deserving exceptional treatment as aggravating or mitigating factors that would affect the classification and punishment of those who commit homicide.[62] Regardless of the procedure adopted for legal reform, Silving insists that the law should be informed by such basic moral principles as the equal value of human life and the freedom of each person.[63]

The principle of equality precludes the sacrifice of one life, however useless and burdensome, for the benefit of another, however useful. On the basis of this principle, the law should give no special considerations whatever for euthanasia that is administered for the sake of anyone other than the suffering patient. The principle of freedom affirms the right to choose to live and thus prohibits the taking of a person's life against his wishes. It also implies the right to choose to die and serves as the basis for a moral distinction between voluntary and involuntary euthanasia. Although Silving gives priority to the value of life, she acknowledges the "profound moral difference between euthanasia administered at the patient's own request and acts done of the actor's 'own hand.' " [64] The Norwegian Penal Code, which makes possible lighter penalties for mercy killing upon request, is recommended as an example of the way in which the law can take this distinction into account. The difference between assisting suicides and instigating suicide is also suggested as a basis for distinguishing between cases in which euthanasia is performed at the patient's request and those in which it is practiced merely with his consent or in response to a request instigated by someone else.

Silving argues that such statutory provisions to reduce the penalty for mercy killing are the most appropriate solutions to the legal problems that now result from its practice. She offers three primary reasons for this conclusion:

a. The method of reducing the penalty of homicide in the case of mercy killing has the advantage of not being objectionable from a religious point of view. For religions do not deny that there are degrees of sin or guilt depending on the underlying motive and that punishment ought to be differentiated in accordance with these.

b. Reduction of penalty in the case of homicide motivated by mercy merely presupposes the assumption that such an act is less reprehensible than an ordinary act of homicide. There is no evidence that the majority of the American people approve of euthanasia, but it is reasonable to assume that most people consider a killing motivated by mercy less reprehensible than killing for a base motive.

c. The European experience with the separate crime of "homicide upon request" does not warrant apprehension of abuse. The danger of abuse would be further decreased by addition of the qualifying fact of incurable illness of the deceased.[65]

There are at least two important reasons for criticizing Silving's proposals for legal reform as not thoroughgoing enough. In the first place, they call for the application of norms and penalties consistent with "the prevailing mores of American society." [66] In cases involving hopeless suffering, however, the basic value commitments of those involved come into fundamental conflict, establish different priorities, and make demands that are incompatible with the value orientation underlying these legal standards. Appropriate laws for cases involving euthanasia should take into account the tensions between the customary values and requirements of society and the claims of suffering and dying patients. Attempts to reform the law should strive to preserve the one without denying the validity of the other. In the second place, a legal system that only reduces the penalty for euthanasia is not sufficient to meet the problems of contemporary medical practice in terminal cases, because it fails to provide adequate guidelines for the difficult life and death decisions that must be made in this context. Silving suggests that perhaps voluntary passive euthanasia should not be punished when it is motivated by the physician's desire not to prolong suffering. This would not be adequate unless *nonfeasance* is interpreted broadly enough to include the active termination of artificial life-sustaining measures. In such cases active and passive euthanasia would not be as "clearly distinguishable" as Silving implies, and the doctor would still be required to act at his own peril in order to alleviate suffering.

There are numerous factors to take into account in order to determine appropriate medical and legal policies with regard to the question of euthanasia. On the one hand, it is necessary to understand the problems that arise and the technical options that are available in the context of terminal medical practice. On the other hand, it is important to be aware of the difficulties of structuring and applying legal standards for medical practice, especially in cases involving hopeless suffering. To overcome these problems, it is necessary to consider the various alternatives within our legal system. Furthermore, responsible guidelines for medical decisions and for legal norms relative to terminal medical care require insight into the meaning of basic ethical values and principles.

6

NEW REQUIREMENTS
OF CARE FOR THE DYING

In the context of growing religious and moral pluralism, many controversial moral questions are left open for individual solutions. Such freedom is often appropriate when the consequences of personal choices are limited and the rights of others are not threatened. This is not the case, however, with decisions having to do with the practice of euthanasia. Professional medical ethics and legal codes serve to protect the lives of patients from arbitrary decisions by those who are entrusted with their care. The validity of these traditional moral norms is challenged by questions of a person's right to die and a doctor's right to allow or to cause his death in hopeless cases to end useless suffering.

These questions must be resolved in order to maintain acceptable standards for terminal medical care. If, on the one hand, patients do not have the right to die rather than to endure hopeless suffering, then moral and legal norms should be established and enforced to prevent the furtive practice of euthanasia. On the other hand, if patients have not only the right to live but also the right to die, then moral and legal codes should be revised to permit them to choose to die and to allow doctors to act on this request. Appropriate standards should be formulated for the protection of both patients and physicians.

CHRISTIAN MEDICAL ETHICS

The principles and moral norms of Christian medical ethics stem from a fundamental commitment of faith in God. This constitutes the primary distinction between Christian ethics and secular ethics which is based on finite centers of value. According to H. Richard Niebuhr, the Christian faith begins with "the transcendent One for whom alone there is ultimate good and for whom, as the source and end of all things, whatever is, is good." [1] On this basis, it constructs and orders relative systems of value. Theocentric faith rejects those systems which absolutize finite values. Thus it challenges the value systems that some legal and professional standards of medical practice make absolute.

Unlike finite centers of value, the ultimate value center of monotheism is not itself an object of value. In Niebuhr's terms, it is the "One beyond the many." [2] This center of value is the source of being and value by virtue of which all that is finite exists and has value. Faith in this transcendent One is a personal response to God as Creator, Lord, and Redeemer. In this response, man recognizes the meaning and scope of ethical responsibility. What is required of him is a total and realistic response to the claim of God and to the needs and claims of his neighbors. Each of these dimensions of man's responsibility must be taken into account in order to provide guidelines for responsible medical care for patients who are suffering and dying.

The response of faith to the creating, judging, and redeeming love of God is responsive love. In response to God as Creator, faithful love embraces the entire universe as it is created by God. Furthermore, it engages in the creative work of God in the world. In the practice of medicine, this love expresses itself in responsible care for human life. It provides medical care for patients who are defective as well as for those who are normal, for the living as well as for the dying. Such care is responsible to God and is responsive to the needs of each patient as a person.

As medical science and technology advance, man's freedom in relation to the processes of life and death is extended. This freedom can be used to prolong life and to preserve the dignity and personhood that makes life human. At the same time, however, this freedom can be used simply to prolong life without regard for its quality and dignity. In the exercise of this freedom, responsible medical care is person-oriented. Thus, in deciding the appropriate course of treatment, it gives personal considerations priority over medical considerations in each case.

Faith in God as sovereign Lord acknowledges that man's freedom and responsibility in relation to the created order are not unlimited. In response to the love of God, faithful love accepts the limitations that he imposes. Furthermore, it engages in the work of God within the limits and possibilities of human existence. In responsible medical care, death is one of the limitations that must be taken into account. When death is interpreted as the enemy of life, its inevitability is often denied, and efforts to prolong life tend to take priority over care for the patient who is suffering and dying. Theocentric faith, however, understands death as one of the processes of life as it is created and sustained by God. From this perspective, it recognizes that there is no absolute right or duty to postpone death. Furthermore, love that is responsible to God is free to provide medical care that corresponds with the needs of each patient.

Responsible love expresses itself not only in concrete decisions and actions but also in ethical principles and moral norms. As Paul Ramsey points out, "obedience to the divine command through love of neighbor can and may and must be prolonged into specifiable requirements for the respect, preservation and protection of life for love to have any significant meaning or relevance." [3] Responsive love always begins with the needs and claims of the neighbor as an individual in society. On the basis of its insight and experience, it formulates universal principles and particular rules and guidelines in order to delineate the requirements of love. Because of the destruction and suffering caused by man's lack of responsibility, responsible love engages in the ordering work of God through established standards of morality, systems of laws, and structures of justice. At the same time, however, it recognizes that these are human institutions which are subject to divine judgment.

Faith in God as Redeemer transforms all of man's responses, for it frees him from fear and despair to care for his neighbor. The love of God, which reconciles man with God, redeems man from the need for self-justification. Thus, it grants him the freedom to respond to the claims of others and even to incur guilt for their sakes. This freedom is especially important when there are no clearly good alternatives and the consequences of any decision are uncertain. It is necessary for responsible medical care when the requirements of love conflict with conventional moral and legal standards of medical practice. In response to the redeeming love of God, love that is responsive to the needs and claims of the patient is free to bear the responsibility for those of its decisions and actions which violate these standards. It also seeks to reform moral and legal norms in the light of the requirements of responsible medical care.

As Redeemer, God frees man not only from guilt and the fear of guilt but also from the fear of death. As Niebuhr points out, "redemption appears as the liberty to interpret in trust all that happens as contained within an intention and a total activity that includes death within the domain of life, that destroys only to re-establish and renew." [4] The implications of this freedom for terminal medical care are significant. In response to the redeeming love of God, a person who is dying can confront death without anxiety or despair. In fact, he may welcome death as a merciful release from suffering. Furthermore, those who care for him can accept the fact that he is dying and enable him to die with dignity.

This perspective provides a basis for criticizing two of the most common approaches to terminal medical care. In the first place, many doctors adopt a policy of prolonging life as long as possible, as if physical life were the only value to be taken into account in responsible medical care. This assumption must be challenged by theocentric love which is responsive to the personal as well as the medical needs of patients. In the second place, doctors often seek to avoid responsibility for terminal medical decisons by simply placing the care of dying patients "in the hands of God." Their failure to provide appropriate care for the dying constitutes a defection from their responsibility to the patient. This must be rejected in response to God, whose love embraces not only the living but also the dying.

Opposition to active and passive euthanasia in terminal medical care also must be questioned from the point of view of theocentric love. In professional medical ethics, euthanasia is opposed on the basis of criminal laws against homicide and on the basis of a vitalistic regard for life as the highest value. In traditional theological ethics, this limitation on the permissible practices for a patient's care is based on the Biblical commandment "Thou shalt not kill." In order not to violate these injunctions in caring for patients who are suffering and dying, it is necessary to distinguish between killing and allowing to die. This distinction is often difficult to make both from a medical and from a moral perspective. Furthermore, it does not provide a basis for permitting passive euthanasia, for *deliberately* allowing a patient to die in order to end his suffering is morally and legally equivalent to direct killing.

Although a theocentric medical ethic values life as it is created and sustained by God, it is fundamentally patient-oriented rather than life-oriented. Thus it rejects absolutistic medical and legal norms against the practice of euthanasia because they place more importance on the life of the patient than on his personal needs and claims. A theocentric medical ethic also challenges vitalistic interpretations of the Sixth Commandment that rule out the practice of euthanasia. In *The New English Bible*, this commandment is translated as "You shall not commit murder" rather than as "You shall not kill." This more accurate translation is consistent with the way in which the commandment is interpreted in the Sermon on the Mount. From the perspective of theocentric faith, it has important implications for terminal medical care.

Under the commandment "Do not murder," there is no moral distinction between killing and allowing to die. The primary moral question concerns the motive or intention underlying the action or the omission that results in death. To allow a person to die out of malice or from disregard is as morally wrong as it is to take his life maliciously. To take a patient's life in order to end his suffering, however, may be as morally justifiable as to allow him to die out of mercy. From the point of view of a person-oriented medical ethic, the patient's right to choose to live or to die is a crucial factor insofar as the morality of euthanasia is concerned. Just as it is morally wrong to take his life or to allow him to die arbitrarily, it may be wrong to prolong his life against his will. Furthermore, to take a patient's life at his request and to relieve his suffering may be as morally right as to allow him to die under the same conditions. In fact, there may be cases in which active euthanasia is more merciful and therefore more justifiable than passive euthanasia.

GUIDELINES FOR MEDICAL PRACTICE

There is little question concerning the requirements of responsible medical care when a physician can offer the hope of recovery or can prolong life without undue suffering. Under these circumstances, there are several general responsibilities that seldom conflict. In the first place, there is a duty to recognize the autonomy of each patient. So long as a person is competent, decisions should not be made and treatment rendered without his informed consent. In the second place, every available means should be offered to restore his health or to preserve his life as long as possible. In the third place, the doctor should alleviate suffering and secure the most rewarding life for each patient.

In numerous cases, these duties and expectations conflict. Efforts to prolong the patient's life frequently result in the prolongation of his suffering and dying. Measures to provide the necessary relief often precipitate his death. This moral dilemma, however, can be resolved when those who are responsible for the patient's care are attentive to his needs and desires. If he is able, the patient should be allowed to determine the course of treatment to be followed. Otherwise, someone else must be prepared to make this decision in his behalf. In either case, the physician has a responsibility to counsel both the patient and his family in order to help them cope with the problem.

1. Sharing the Burden of Responsibility

Patients who are suffering and dying usually cannot make responsible medical decisions on their own. In the majority of cases, the responsibility for their care rests entirely on their families or their doctors. In a complex and mobile society, however, familial relationships are often tenuous and undependable. Furthermore, because the practice of medicine is highly specialized, the doctor-patient relationship tends to be technical and impersonal. These are factors that must be taken into account in guidelines for terminal medical decisions.

In the place of the conventional pattern of private practice, a social systems model provides a more inclusive perspective from which to interpret the structure of medical practice. From this point of view, the moral and the legal responsibilities of the physician can be defined. The doctor-patient relationship is a unit or a subsystem that is part and parcel of a larger system of interrelated collectivities. On the one hand, this dyadic relationship is a minimal-level system. It constitutes an adequate basis for medical practice in emergency situations and in routine cases when the bearing of other related systems is insignificant insofar as medical decisions are concerned. On the other hand, the doctor and the patient are members of a larger social system. This frame of reference is important in cases of serious injury or illness and when medical resources are expensive or limited. In such cases, a plurality of needs and interests impinge on the therapeutic relationship.

This analysis exposes a cross section of the relationships in which both doctors and patients are involved in terminal medical care. These relationships provide the basis on which they can share the burden of responsibility for the decisions that must be made in this context. Teams of doctors and clergy, psychiatrists and counselors, along with members of other professions, including nurses, social workers, and lawyers, can contribute insight and can assure that terminal decisions are made at a high level of integrity. Through discussions and counseling, the physician can enable the patient and his family to understand the diagnosis and the prognosis. Counselors and psychiatrists can help the dying patient preserve his identity and dignity as a unique individual, despite the disease. They can also attend the living and help them to overcome feelings of anxiety, resentment, and guilt and to adjust to their loss. Chaplains and clergymen often can foster communication, assist the doctor in understanding the patient's beliefs and desires, and help both physicians and patients to find meaning and values that transcend suffering and death.

The primary purpose of interdisciplinary cooperation and understanding is to assure that every patient is offered the opportunity to live as long and as fully as possible and is given an appropriate emotional world in which to die. It is essential for cases in which the only relevant medical resources are limited, or experimental, or in which they promise little hope and cause undue suffering or expense. Such teamwork is particularly important when a patient's condition is irremediable and it becomes necessary to redirect the skills of medicine in order to preserve his dignity, to relieve suffering, and to make possible an easy death. This procedure is fitting in a wide variety of circumstances, especially when disease or the degenerative processes of age progress too far or when injury or deformity is too radical to permit even a limited but choice-worthy existence. In such cases, three alternatives remain within which specific courses of action must be determined:

  a. *Prolongation of life* involves ameliorative and emergency treatment in order to sustain life as long as possible. Although supportive efforts are given priority, palliative measures are applied to make the limited remaining life as comfortable as possible. All remedial treatment that causes distress is omitted.

b. *Passive euthanasia* includes palliative therapy and limited ameliorative treatment in order to relieve suffering without prolonging life. Emergency and remedial procedures are omitted and supportive measures are reduced to allow the patient to die.

c. *Active euthanasia* entails the application of palliative treatment and deliberate measures to cause death. In extreme cases, the borderline between passive and active euthanasia is often very subtle, both in intention and in action. Direct action to end life may involve administering lethal pain-killers or terminating artificial supportive measures, for example, turning off a respirator or a heart-lung machine.

2. General Guidelines for Medical Decisions

When it becomes apparent that medical care ought to be restricted to one of these levels, every aspect of the case should be examined thoroughly, and each decision should be endorsed by a committee of medical and nonmedical specialists. This committee would be analogous to panels that are created to approve abortions and to select patients for treatment when facilities are limited. The authority of such committees should be strictly limited, but they should have the following responsibilities:

a. To guarantee each patient's right to live and his right to die.

b. To verify the doctor's diagnosis and to protect him from false and dangerous criticism.

c. To offer advice and understanding to patient and family.

d. To assure that hope for recovery and efforts to prolong life are not given up prematurely.

e. To document each case as carefully as possible in order to prevent irresponsible decisions.

Committees that are responsible for evaluating terminal medical care should have at least five members. They should include no fewer than two physicians in fields related to the patient's condition. These doctors should not be related to him in any other way, directly or indirectly, as members of his family, as his personal physician, or as doctors connected with cases for which he might be regarded as a donor of vital organs. A representative of the hospital administration should be on these committees to assure that the policies of the hospital are followed. Furthermore, such committees should include a counselor or psychiatrist and a chaplain or the patient's rabbi, priest, or minister. Any other person requested by the patient or his family should be allowed to participate in the deliberations and the decisions of the committee.

Responsibility to a patient as a person requires that he be permitted to make his own medical decisions. Thus, so long as he is conscious and competent, medical care should neither be applied nor denied without his knowledge and consent. The mere fact that he is terminally ill or fatally injured and suffering does not undermine the value of his life or relieve the obligation of family and physician to care for him. In many cases, a desperate hope for recovery, or deep personal relationships, or important goals yet to be fulfilled add meaning and purpose to the brief time that remains. Therefore involuntary euthanasia should never be permitted.

The fact that a patient places himself and remains under the care of a doctor does not indicate implied consent to any and every therapeutic measure. Furthermore, the fact that he wants to die does not in itself indicate a mental condition that renders him incompetent to make his own medical decisions. Those who are responsible for his care must make certain that he is fully capable of understanding his condition and that his request to die is an expression of

his genuine and consistent desire. Nevertheless, when a
patient wishes to die and his suffering cannot be relieved
adequately or his condition renders his life hopelessly
intolerable, he should be permitted to refuse treatment to
prolong his life. In extreme cases, he should even be
allowed to choose measures to end his life directly. In short,
voluntary euthanasia, both active and passive, ought to be
sanctioned in response to the needs and claims of the dying.

For the patient who is unconscious or incompetent, the
family or guardian usually assumes a much greater role in
determining the course of medical care. In such cases, a
committee is especially important to assure that they fully
understand the patient's condition, that the treatment that
doctors can offer is explained, and that their decisions are
made in the patient's best interest. The fact that someone
else had to decide in his behalf in no way undermines the
value of his life, and so long as recovery is possible, even if it
is only limited or temporary recovery, his right to live
should be preserved. This does not imply that a person's life
should be prolonged at all costs simply because he is not
able to make his own decisions, but it underscores the
seriousness of interrupting therapy aimed at recovery or
prolongation of life.

In the course of prescribing care for an incompetent
patient, the problem of suffering should be taken into
consideration. It is irresponsible to require a person to
endure useless emotional or physical distress simply because
he is not able to give informed consent either to the
withdrawal of efforts to prolong his life or to measures to
cause his death. Consequently, the patient who loses
consciousness or experiences cardiac arrest often should not
be revived simply to undergo hopeless suffering. Through
consultation with doctors and counselors, his family should
be informed concerning his condition. Their questions and
uncertainties should be resolved, and they should be

prepared to choose or to share the responsibility of deciding whether or not to continue to prolong his life.

In making terminal medical decisions, the extent to which vital systems have been destroyed by accident or by disease should be evaluated thoroughly. It is not always possible to determine this with absolute certainty; nevertheless, there are clinical tests which are indispensable. According to Dr. Hannibal Hamlin, "the EEG can signal a point of no return, although the cardiovascular system continues to respond to supportive therapy that produces a respectable ECG." [5] Dr. Denton Cooley has reported that there is a general agreement among the surgeons who have performed heart transplants concerning three criteria for declaring a patient dead in addition to a flat EEG: the patient should no longer have natural heartbeat, respiration, or reflex.[6] These clinical signs of brain death have also been recommended by a committee of the Harvard Medical School under the chairmanship of Dr. Henry K. Beecher.[7]

The way in which these signs are interpreted reflects the way in which death is defined within the medical profession. Increasingly, "brain death" is replacing the traditional definition of death as the permanent absence of respiration and circulation. The same criteria are applied, however, because respiratory and to some degree cardiovascular activities are functions of the brain stem. In addition to conventional tests for death, the electroencephalograph provides confirmatory data.[8] When these tests reveal the absence of spontaneous signs of life, all of the so-called life-sustaining measures should be terminated.

In most cases involving permanently comatose patients, brain damage is not serious enough to warrant declaring the patient dead as the basis for discontinuing medical treatment. Terminal decisions in these cases tend to be especially difficult. Although it may be pointless to sustain the life of a patient in this condition, relatives and physicians are usually reluctant to do otherwise. At the same time, the irretrievably unconscious patient is totally unable to respond to their care. In fact, he lacks even the potential for personal relationships which make life human. In such cases, as Ramsey has observed, "the duty always to keep caring for the dying is suspended by their inaccessibility to any form of care and comfort." [9] Furthermore, it makes no difference, insofar as the patient is concerned, whether his death is brought about by passive or active means.

3. Guidelines Concerning Defective Infants

The ideal solution to the problem of birth defects is, of course, to prevent them altogether, but our knowledge of their genetic sources is insufficient to reduce seriously the frequency of malformations. The discovery of abnormalities after conception has been limited because of the dangerous level of radiation exposure required for X-ray examinations;[10] nevertheless, other diagnostic procedures, such as prenatal chromosome studies, offer good prospects of early detection. In this event and when there is evidence of radical deformity as the result of an infection, such as rubella, or following the consumption of a teratogenic agent, such as thalidomide, abortion may be indicated. At the present time, however, this approach is applicable in only a relatively few cases, for most abnormalities remain unsuspected until after birth and are not caused by disease or by toxic drugs.[11]

As a general rule in responsible medical practice, it is the child which matters and not the parents when the application of a particular treatment is in question.[12] This rule is also relevant for the care of most defective children, for an increasing majority are able to lead useful and rewarding lives. It is especially applicable for cases in which it is not possible to determine early in life the extent or consequences of a recognized defect. When the child involved is severely defective, however, the wishes and desires of the parents should be taken into account. The difficult decisions concerning the proper course to follow must still give priority to the welfare of the child. They cannot be made on the basis of the parents' interests alone. Furthermore, the question should not be resolved by appeal to expedience, economic necessity, or the good of society at large. In short, responsible medical care cannot condone euthanasia as a eugenic measure.

A second general rule of medical practice requires that the abnormal patient be given the same quality of care as the normal patient.[13] This also should apply to "normal" children with specific defects of intellectual function and for those of normal intelligence with physical abnormalities, such as talipes, polydactylism, cleft lip, cleft palate, and remediable cardiac malformations. These conditions may have relatively little effect on the quality of life, and in the course of these lives much more can be done to ameliorate the consequences of such defects.[14] Obviously, the desirability of continued existence under these circumstances cannot be seriously questioned. With regard to deformities caused by thalidomide, for example, Drs. Charles H. Franz and George T. Aiken insist that we would be defeatists to consider euthanasia for phocomelic children. "The proponents of this procedure," they argue, "fail to realize that many of these children are of normal and high normal intelligence, indicating an excellent possibility of emotional and social habilitation." [15]

In contrast with these, for whom doctors and parents should assume the responsibility of securing the maximum possible quality of life, there are infrequent cases of gross physical deformities (such as major cardiac abnormalities) and severe defects of the central nervous system (for example, anencephalus) for which there can be little or no hope of survival. Between these two extremes is a range of conditions that are severely defective—mentally or physically, or both. These often raise difficult questions concerning the desirability and the effectiveness of medical intervention. The following three kinds of abnormalities illustrate the medical dimensions of this dilemma:

a. Spina bifida is a relatively common defect which poses this problem more acutely, perhaps, than any other condition. The majority of infants with this condition die without treatment or in spite of it, but in a few cases modern medical and surgical procedures can offer a chance of reasonably normal life. On the other hand, the risk is great that the child will remain paralyzed for the rest of his life.[16]

b. Mongolism is a second syndrome that often poses difficult medical and moral problems. Once again, early mortality is high, usually as a result of cardiac and other serious malformations, but it is not uncommon for mongols to survive to adult life and even old age.[17] Although physically deformed and mentally subnormal, many are able to enjoy life, and so long as their condition does not deprive them of this value, life should not be denied them simply because they are unable to conceptualize their desires. Nevertheless, they should not be required to endure needless suffering; and when this occurs, or when radical corrective treatment is required, decisions must be rendered in their behalf by those entrusted with their care.

c. Hydrocephalus is a third common type of serious abnormality which requires appropriate surgical measures in order to increase the chance of survival and minimize disability. Without treatment approximately half of the hydrocephalic infants that are live-born die within five years,[18] and those that survive usually suffer severe deformities, such as an enormously unsightly head, mental and neurologic damage, and progressive optic atrophy.[19] While surgical intervention often limits and occasionally prevents damage, it also greatly increases the possibility that the patient whose life is saved will be radically disabled.[20]

For any of these conditions, it is not responsible practice simply to postpone decisions and allow the patient to die rather than to face the alternatives and consequences and to choose an appropriate response to the needs of the patient and those intimately related to him. The doctor should not be expected to shoulder the full responsibility for determining the proper course to follow. As in cases in which the patient is unconscious or otherwise incapable of giving informed consent to medical decisions, the physician can provide the necessary information concerning the condition of the defective child and recommend one or several alternatives. A committee of specialists in several fields can offer insight and guidance. In the last analysis, however, the primary responsibility for decisions belongs to the parents.

4. Guidelines Concerning the Aged

Age *per se* has nothing at all to do with the quality and value of life, and the experience, the wisdom, and the relationships that most people develop throughout their lives often make the advancing years most rewarding. Improved environmental conditions and health care enable many to remain well and self-sufficient beyond the Biblical threescore and ten years. Even though the incidence of chronic disease is high among persons over sixty-five, much can be done to ameliorate their conditions, and with

patience and proper treatment, the majority of elderly
incapacitated persons can eventually be rehabilitated.
Therefore, necessary medical and surgical care should not
be denied merely because of advanced age.

The term "aged" is for all practical purposes a physiological rather than a chronological concept. In this sense, age is
often an important criterion for determining how long to
prolong life and when to apply heroic measures. Younger
patients usually have a much greater chance of withstanding
serious illness and recovering from critical injury. In cases
of cerebral accidents, for example, they are often able to
make satisfactory recovery even after a long period of
unconsciousness, because the brain has a remarkable capacity to compensate for injury. For older patients, however,
this possibility is very slight, especially when their condition
stems from cerebrovascular diseases.

When a cure could offer the prospects of a reasonably full
life, the rapid pace of medical research and the hope for
new life-saving measures usually warrant efforts to prolong
the lives of patients who are presently incurable. For the
very elderly who are afflicted with advanced cardiovascular,
cerebrovascular, or malignant diseases this support may not
be justifiable, especially when suffering is involved. Furthermore, if they must endure severe, intractable pain from
rheumatoid arthritis, for instance, it might on occasion be
more merciful to terminate treatment for intercurrent
infections such as pneumonia, which Dr. William Osler used
to call "the old man's friend." [21]

So long as the patient is capable, he should always be
allowed to determine the goal toward which care should be
directed and the measures that should be applied. Dr.
Walter C. Alvarez, emeritus consultant at the Mayo Clinic,
points out that

> with these old persons who have suffered long, the physician
> is usually safe in discussing death and dying. With such

persons he need fear no embarrassment about mentioning these things. The patient will show little fear, and all he may ask of his physician is that he prevent suffering at the end.[22]

When the elderly patient cannot make this decision, Dr. Alvarez suggests

that the relatives should be asked if they wish the physician to keep carrying out efforts at resuscitation with much oxygen and endless injections of stimulants, or if they would prefer to let the loved one pass peacefully when his or her time has come. Sometimes, as in the case of a patient suffering from a brain tumor, the physician should point out that even if through some miracle he could prolong life for a few weeks, the person would be so badly crippled in mind and body that he or she would be utterly miserable and perhaps in constant pain. Often the family knows that the patient would be better off dead, but they do not have the courage to say this, fearing that they would be criticized by someone.[23]

In every case, a team of competent physicians and counselors should assist the patient, his family, and his doctor in making the difficult decisions required by suffering and death.

MEDICAL ETHICS IN A PLURALISTIC SOCIETY

Theocentric love does not begin with general or abstract principles from which to deduce specific moral norms for medical care. Instead, it begins with the concrete needs of patients as persons. It seeks to understand and to respond to the needs and claims of each patient in the context of a society that is increasingly complex. In specific cases, responsible love takes into account the long-range results, as well as the immediate consequences, of its decisions and actions. On the basis of its insight and experience, i formulates moral norms that are relevant to the problems o contemporary medical practice.

When the requirements of love conflict with medical and legal standards of practice, responsible love seeks to reform these moral norms. In order to change accepted moral rule in a pluralistic society, it is necessary to locate a basis fo agreement on the level of ethical values and principles Daniel Callahan suggests that the principle of the sanctity of life provides the basis for a moral consensus from which to evaluate and to affirm or to amend moral standard having to do with human control over life and death.[24] It i important to recognize, however, that the logic of mora discourse is not a strictly deductive science. Furthermore such ethical concepts are indeterminate principles which convey broad ranges of meaning rather than specific determinate meanings.[25] In fact, the "sanctity of life" i interpreted in a number of different ways in our society Thus an appeal to this generic principle does not *entai* specific moral conclusions.

This principle is often understood to imply that life *per se* is of ultimate value. Professional medical ethics tends to give priority to the value of biological life and to order other values and obligations accordingly. Because they are usu ally compatible, these values make possible standards o practice that are relatively consistent and applicable in most cases. These standards require that doctors secure the maximum longevity possible. So long as a patient can be cured or at least offered a reasonably full life, the doctor's responsibility to work toward this end is seldom challenged When this goal becomes unrealistic, however, his duty to prolong life as long as possible can be called into question Nevertheless, traditional legal and professional medica standards strictly forbid him to practice euthanasia.

For many people, including both doctors and laymen, the

sanctity of life often seems to be destroyed by desperate efforts to prolong life in the face of hopeless suffering. They interpret this principle to refer to more than mere biological existence. From their perspective, a terminal patient's request to die is not always considered to be irresponsible. Furthermore, a doctor's decision to omit resuscitative procedures, to suspend supportive measures, or to prescribe lethal pain-killers is not necessarily regarded as a violation of the sanctity of life. In some cases, such omissions and actions appear to reflect a reappraisal of the meaning of this principle in the light of new medical options and human needs and as a reassessment of the implicit moral norms for terminal medical decisions.

The sanctity of life is often judged in relation to other ethical principles. When it is contigent upon the quality of life, the doctor is not required to prolong life indefinitely after the quality of life has been undermined by suffering, age, deformity, injury, or illness. If he cannot cure, he may be called upon to ease suffering by every possible means, including euthanasia. When the sanctity of life is based upon its worth to society, a doctor may not be expected to "save" patients who have no social value. If there are heavy demands on limited medical personnel and facilities, he may choose to allow the "hopeless" and the "useless" to die prematurely in order to make space and treatment available for other patients. In the last analysis, medical care is provided only for "life that is worth living" when either hedonistic or utilitarian principles constitute the primary basis for the moral norms of medical practice.

Within Christian medical ethics, the sanctity of life is a basic ethical principle. Underlying this principle, however, is a fundamental commitment to God as the ultimate source of being and value. On the basis of this commitment, theocentric faith affirms and orders ethical values and moral norms. It also rejects those systems which absolutize finite centers of value. Consequently, this faith challenges the vitalism implicit in legal and professional standards of medical practice. Furthermore, it opposes hedonism and utilitarianism as bases for medical ethics.

Unlike these secular faiths, theocentric faith interprets the principle of the sanctity of life in relation to God as Creator, Lord, and Redeemer. It emphasizes the importance of the physical-biological dimension of a person's existence and the significance of the sociocultural matrix of his life. Nevertheless, these factors are not the source of life or of its sacredness. As a basic principle of Christian ethics, the sanctity of life affirms a person's right to live and safeguards this right against the conflicting values and claims of society. At the same time, this principle does not translate this right into a necessity. From the perspective of Christian faith, the sanctity of life is not destroyed by death, for death is understood as a process of life as it is created and sustained by God.

Respect for the sanctity of life constitutes the basis of many of the professional and legal standards of medical practice. The way in which this principle is interpreted from the point of view of theocentric faith has important implications for medical care. It also provides a basis for transforming the moral norms governing the practice of medicine. Because there is a general consensus within our society concerning this principle, Christian medical ethics finds areas of basic agreement with regard to its meaning in terms of responsible medical care. Where there are differences of opinion, as is the case with the question of euthanasia, Christian ethics seeks to foster a more profound consensus on the basis of its understanding of the meaning of the sanctity of life. Agreement on this level would make it possible to transform traditional standards of terminal medical care in keeping with the requirements of responsible medical practice.

GUIDELINES FOR LEGAL NORMS

Innovations in medical science and technology often create complex moral dilemmas. This in turn makes it especially difficult to change laws that have to do with the practice of medicine. Questions that arise in the context of terminal medical care cannot be answered solely on the basis of the rules of the past or on the basis of prevailing medical and legal practices. Although these factors should be taken into account, new standards with which to resolve these problems must be derived from the fundamental ethical values underlying our moral and legal norms. Thus it is necessary to reexamine the meaning of these principles in the light of the new options that are available in medical practice.

1. Updating the Concept of Death

Death is a social as well as a private event and a legal as well as a medical question. Nevertheless, legal and medical definitions of death no longer coincide. The legal concept of death is quite general and does not take into account the changes that have occurred in the practice of medicine. Courts, for example, usually interpret death simply as a state that is the antithesis of life and as an event that takes place at a specific point in time when vital functions cease and can no longer be revived.[26] From this perspective, a patient is considered to be alive as long as any heartbeat and respiration can be perceived with or without instruments, regardless of how these signs of life are maintained.[27]

The medical concept of death is much more complex, for doctors understand death as a dynamic process rather than as a single event. Their distinction between *organismic* or *clinical* death (the loss of vital functions, which is sometimes reversible) and *organic* or *medical* death (the death of all systems, which is final) should be taken seriously in efforts to update legal definitions of death. This is especially important because of the possibility of prolonging the signs of life long after the loss of vital functions is permanent. The ability to save lives by means of organ transplants also makes it necessary to have a legal definition of death that distinguishes between organismic and organic death.

Irreversible cerebral failure has been suggested as an indication of death. In fact, courts and legislatures are increasingly taking this medical concept of death into account. Several states—for example, Kansas, Maryland, and California—have already enacted legislative changes to include brain death in addition to permanent cessation of respiration and circulation in legal definitions of death. This should not be interpreted as an expression of a sophisticated vitalism. When the principle of the sanctity of life is understood in human terms rather than with reference to biological existence alone, brain death seems to be an appropriate basis for a legal as well as a medical definition of death. As Dr. Hamlin points out, "the sanctity of life is not generated by cardiac signs of its presence or absence when the brain has already died." [28]

The life of the brain is an indispensable dimension of human existence. Respect for a patient's life and responsibility to him as a person require that every reasonable means to prolong life be offered as long as his brain survives. To amend conventional legal concepts of death to include neurological death would allow doctors to introduce artificial life-sustaining measures without the obligation to continue their use indefinitely. Clinical tests that determine when irreversible brain death has occurred would provide criteria for declaring a patient dead. This would also enable doctors to "save" essential organs from donors in order to prolong the lives of other patients. In the last analysis, however, the greatest care should be taken and safeguards should be established to assure that death is declared because a patient is dead and not because he is a donor.

2. Sanctions for Passive Euthanasia

The law seeks to protect each person's right to live. Furthermore, it does not recognize mercy as a legitimate excuse or justification for homicide. Thus there are no sanctions for active or passive euthanasia against a patient's will (involuntary euthanasia). Theoretically, in the absence of mitigating circumstances, involuntary euthanasia is a felony. When it is committed intentionally, as in the case of a deliberate overdose of a lethal narcotic, it reflects a willful disregard for the victim's right to life. Because of the sanctity of each patient as a person, this should be defined as murder and punished accordingly. When involuntary euthanasia is performed unintentionally, as in the case of an accidental overdose of a lethal narcotic, it should be treated as involuntary manslaughter or negligent homicide. The fact that the patient's life is not taken deliberately provides the rationale for the lesser charge. At the same time, however, this provision would serve to protect patients from negligence.

In addition to the right to life, the law guarantees personal autonomy so long as an individual's exercise of his freedom does not interfere with the rights or the freedom of others. The right of each person to make his own medical decisions, for example, is protected even when his life is at stake. Except in emergencies, the doctor's right to act in order to help or to save is strictly limited by the patient's right to refuse his services. This, however, enables the doctor to practice passive euthanasia, for he must refrain from efforts to prolong life when a patient refuses to consent. At the same time, he may yield to the patient's request and direct his attention fully toward relieving suffering and preparing both the patient and the family for death.

When it is understood in personal terms, respect for the sanctity of life involves a recognition of the freedom of each individual. In the practice of medicine, this respect requires that the patient be permitted to determine the course of the medical treatment that he receives. There are circumstances, however, in which a person's wishes cannot be known or must be disregarded. When, for example, a patient is not competent to give or to withhold consent, the doctor is not bound by his refusal of necessary treatment. In such cases, medical decisions are usually made by the doctor in conjunction with the patient's closest relative or his guardian. Nevertheless, the principle that each person is the master of his own body is important and should be preserved in the law. On this basis, there should be legislation to sanction passive euthanasia.

3. Justification for Active Euthanasia

A good case can also be made for sanctioning active euthanasia. There are occasions in which the patient's desire to live is undermined by suffering and disease even though his death is not imminent. Out of regard for his freedom over his own life and death, he should be allowed to choose to die by active means rather than to endure hopeless suffering. Furthermore, those who assist him should be freed from liability for his death. The moral distinction between killing out of mercy and killing from malice constitutes a basis for distinguishing euthanasia from murder. The extreme leniency that prosecutors, judges, and jurors have accorded those who have killed out of mercy indicates their tacit approval, or at least their acceptance, of active euthanasia in direct opposition to existing laws.

The dangers of errors and abuse are often cited in arguments against legalizing active euthanasia. In the absence of adequate safeguards, such problems would inevitably occur if either a patient's doctor or his family were permitted to practice mercy killing at his request. In some cases, there would be mistakes because of their emotional involvement in the patient's suffering. In other cases, unscrupulous doctors and relatives would take advantage of the law by disguising homicide motivated by greed or enmity as an act of mercy. Because of these dangers, the right to die and the freedom to terminate a patient's life at his request must be limited by conditions that are necessary to secure the right of others to life.

For the good of "society," that is, to protect every patient's right to live, the law should treat active euthanasia as a felony except under legally sanctioned circumstances. Because of the inviolability of each patient, involuntary euthanasia should be defined as murder in the absence of mitigating circumstances. The moral distinction between mercy and malice as motives for homicide provides a basis for declaring unauthorized mercy killing a second-degree felony when it is not in opposition to a patient's desire to live. Although voluntary euthanasia *per se* is not morally reprehensible, it should be defined as manslaughter when it is not performed in accordance with legally prescribed procedures which are designed to preserve both the right to live and the right to die.

Finally, in order to be humane and relevant to the problems that arise in terminal medical care, the law should prescribe conditions that would justify active measures to terminate life and would provide the maximum safety for each patient. Because of the tragic consequences of radical birth defects, advanced degenerative diseases, and hopeless suffering in terminal illness at any age, the right to die should not be denied. Sometimes it is impossible to distinguish between allowing and causing a patient to die on the basis of an objective analysis of the doctor's action. In either case, both the end and the means are the same. After emergency and ameliorative treatment has begun, the doctor must often perform overt acts in order to allow the patient to die. There also may be occasions in which he should be permitted to take direct action to terminate the life of a patient who is not yet on the verge of death.

Legislation establishing legal justifications for voluntary active euthanasia must provide ample safeguards against errors and abuse. Nevertheless, its requirements should not be so complex and restrictive that it would increase the suffering and anxiety of the dying patient and his family. For their safety and for the protection of the doctor, these provisions should be included:

   a. Euthanasia may be justifiable when it is performed at the request of a competent patient whose condition is terminal. When he is permanently incapable of making a request or giving consent to die, his nearest relative or legal guardian may be allowed to act in his behalf. Euthanasia is never justifiable against a person's wishes.
   b. A committee composed of at least five members should evaluate his condition, verify his desire to die, and decide whether active or passive euthanasia is warranted. The committee should include at least two physicians in fields related to the patient's condition, a representative of the hospital administration, a counselor or psychiatrist, and a chaplain, minister, priest, or rabbi. Under no condition should a member of the committee be connected with any case for which the patient might be considered as a donor of organs for transplants.
   c. The patient's condition, his request for euthanasia

(or that of his nearest relative when the patient is incompetent to give informed consent), and the decision of the committee should be indicated on appropriate legal forms, which should be properly attested and recorded.

d. Euthanasia in accordance with these conditions should be defined as a legitimate cause of death and should in no way affect insurance benefits or survivorship rights.

Legislation to permit voluntary active euthanasia in accordance with these regulations would serve to protect each patient's right to die and to preserve his right to live. In the absence of such safeguards, he is dependent upon the moral sensitivity and integrity of those who are responsible for his care. Until there are legal justifications and procedures to allow doctors to practice euthanasia, those who do act out of mercy must in turn rely on the mercy of others who judge their actions. The same moral insight and concern is required in order to reform professional and legal standards of medical practice to make them more responsive to patients who suffering and dying. This challenge must be met by men and women of faith and goodwill in order to exercise wisely and humanely the power over life and death created by contemporary science and technology.

NOTES

Chapter 1. EUTHANASIA: PAST AND PRESENT

1. C. Suetonius Tranquillus, *The Lives of the Twelve Caesars*, tr. by Alexander Thomson (New York: R. Worthington, 1883), pp. 164–165.

2. Francis Bacon, *The Advancement of Learning and Novum Organum* (New York: Colonial Press, 1900), p. 117.

3. Henry E. Sigerist, *A History of Medicine*, Vol. II (Oxford University Press, 1961), p. 32.

4. "The Arts," *Hippocrates*, tr. by W. H. S. Jones (London: William Heinemann, 1923), lines 7–10, p. 193.

5. Emma J. and Ludwig Edelstein, *Asclepius: A Collection and Interpretation of the Testimonies* (Johns Hopkins Press, 1943), Vol. I, p. 169; Vol. II, pp. 44, 309–311.

6. Plato, "The Republic," *The Dialogues of Plato*, Vol. I, tr. by B. Jowett (Random House, 1937), III, 406, p. 670.

7. Strabo, *The Geography of Strabo*, Vol. V, tr. by Horace L. Jones, ed. by T. E. Page *et al.* (The Loeb Classical Library; London: William Heinemann, 1928), X, v, p. 169.

8. Ludwig Edelstein, *The Hippocratic Oath*, Supplements to the *Bulletin of the History of Medicine*, No. 1 (Johns Hopkins Press, 1943), pp. 28–29.

9. E. J. and L. Edelstein, *Asclepius*, Vol. II, p. 123.

10. L. Edelstein, *The Hippocratic Oath*, p. 59.

11. W. Mair, "Suicide: Greek and Roman," *Encyclopedia of*

Religion and Ethics, ed. by James Hastings (Charles Scribner's Sons, 1925), Vol. XII, p. 30.

12. Seneca, *Ad Lucilium Epistulae Morales* (3 vols.), tr. by Richard M. Gummere (London: William Heinemann, 1917), Vol. II, lxx, 8–9, p. 61; cf. Vol. I, xxiv, 22–23, p. 179; xxvi, 7–9, p. 191.

13. Mair, "Suicide: Greek and Roman," *loc. cit.*, p. 30.

14. L. Edelstein, *The Hippocratic Oath*, pp. 14–15.

15. Seneca, *Epistulae Morales*, Vol. I, lvii. 32–36, pp. 407–409.

16. William E. H. Lecky, *History of European Morals* (New York: Appleton, 1895), Vol. II, p. 50.

17. Thomas Aquinas, *The "Summa Theologica" of Saint Thomas Aquinas*, Vol. X, tr. by Fathers of the English Dominican Province (London: Burns, Oates & Washbourne, Ltd., 1929), II, ii, Q. 64, a. 5, pp. 202–205.

18. Martin Luther, *Werke: Tischreden* (Weimar: Hermann Bühlaus Nachfolger, 1919), Vol. V, pp. 8–9.

19. Immanuel Jakobovits, *Jewish Medical Ethics: A Comparative and Historical Study of the Jewish Religious Attitude to Medicine and Its Practice* (Bloch Publishing Company, Inc., 1962), pp. 122; 305, nn. 24, 26, 28; Immanuel Jakobovits, "The Dying and Their Treatment in Jewish Law, Preparation for Death and Euthanasia," *Hebrew Medical Journal*, Vol. XXXIV (1961), p. 247.

20. Dan Mackenzie, "Euthanasia in Folk Medicine in Britain," *The Caledonian Medical Journal*, Vol. XV (October, 1934), p. 306; and David Rorie, "Hastening Death of Aged, Infirm, and Sick," *The British Medical Journal*, Vol. II (Sept. 30, 1933), pp. 611–612.

21. Montaigne, "A Custome of the Isle of Crea," *Essays*, Vol. II (London: J. M. Dent & Sons, Ltd., 1938), p. 27.

22. Bacon, *The Advancement of Learning and Novum Organum*, p. 117.

23. John Donne, *Biathanatos* (The Facsimile Text Society, 1930), pp. 215–216.

24. Carl F. H. Marx, "Medical Euthanasia," tr. by Walter Cane, *Journal of the History of Medicine*, Vol. VII (1952), p. 405.

25. Frank E. Hitchcock, "Euthanasia," *Transactions of the Maine Medical Association*, Vol. X (1889), p. 42.

26. R. F. Rattray, "The Right to Painless Death," *Quarterly Review*, Vol. CCLXXIV (January, 1940), pp. 40–41.

27. Abraham Jacobi, "Euthanasia," *Medical Opinion and Review*, Vol. XVIII (1912), pp. 362–363.

28. "Fortune Survey: Mercy Killings," *Fortune*, Vol. XVI (July, 1937), p. 106.

29. C. Killick Millard, "The Case for Euthanasia," *Fortnightly Review*, Vol. CXX (December, 1930), pp. 708–709.

30. Foster Kennedy, "Euthanasia: To Be or Not to Be," *Colliers*, Vol. CIII (May 20, 1939), p. 15.

31. W. M. Bowman, "Euthanasia," *Virginia Medical Monthly*, Vol. LVI (December, 1939), p. 726.

32. *Ibid.*

33. A. A. Brill, "Reflections on Euthanasia," *Journal of Nervous and Mental Diseases*, Vol. LXXXIV (July, 1936), p. 12.

34. Bowman, "Euthanasia," *loc. cit.*, pp. 726–727.

35. *Ibid.*

36. Helen Silving, "Euthanasia: A Study in Comparative Criminal Law," *University of Pennsylvania Law Review*, Vol. CIII (December, 1954), p. 356, n. 21.

37. *Ibid.*, p. 356, n. 22; Lee Alexander, "Medical Science Under Dictatorship," *The New England Journal of Medicine*, Vol. CCXLI (July 14, 1949), p. 39.

38. Alexander, "Medical Science Under Dictatorship," *loc. cit.*, p. 39.

39. Alexander Mitscherlich and Fred Mielke, *Doctors of Infamy*, tr. by Heinz Norden (Henry Schuman, Inc., Publishers, 1949), p. 90.

40. Silving, "Euthanasia," *loc. cit.*, p. 356, n. 23.

41. Alexander, "Medical Science Under Dictatorship," *loc. cit.*, pp. 39–40; 47, n. 2; Mitscherlich and Mielke, *Doctors of Infamy*, pp. 92–100.

42. Mildred Strunck (ed.), "The Quarters Polls," *The Public Opinion Quarterly*, Vol. XI (Fall, 1947), p. 77.

43. Mildred Strunck (ed.), "The Quarters Polls," *The Public Opinion Quarterly*, Vol. XIV (Feb. 5, 1950), p. 375.

44. Joseph Fletcher, *Medicine and Morals* (Beacon Press, Inc., 1960), pp. 187–188.

45. "Make It Legal?" *Time*, Vol. XLVIII (Nov. 18, 1946), p. 70.

46. *Ibid.*

47. Glanville Williams, *The Sanctity of Life and the Criminal Law* (Alfred A. Knopf, Inc., 1957), p. 332.

48. "Euthanasia," *Facts on File*, Vol. XXXIII (Sept. 23–29, 1973), p. 812.

49. "Majority of Americans Now Say Doctors Should Be Able to Practice Euthanasia," *Gallup Opinion Index* (August, 1973), Report No. 98, pp. 35–36.

Chapter 2. EUTHANASIA: PRO AND CON

1. Henry David Aiken, *Reason and Conduct* (Alfred A. Knopf, Inc., 1962), pp. 66–87.

2. *Principles of Medical Ethics of the American Medical Association* (Chicago: American Medical Association, December, 1964), pp. 5–6.

3. Frank J. Ayd, Jr., "The Hopeless Case," *Journal of the American Medical Association*, Vol. CLXXXI (Sept. 29, 1962), p. 1102.

4. Glanville Williams, *The Sanctity of Life*, p. 331; Glanville Williams, "Mercy Killing Legislation," *Minnesota University Law Review*, Vol. XL (November, 1958), pp. 1–2.

5. Joseph Fletcher, "Our Right to Die," *Theology Today*, Vol. VII (May, 1951), p. 25.

6. Edgar E. Filbey and Kenneth E. Reed, "Some Overtones of Euthanasia," *Hospital Topics*, Vol. XLIII (September, 1965), p. 58.

7. *Hippocrates*, Vol. I, tr. by W. H. S. Jones (The Loeb Classical Library; Harvard University Press, 1962), p. 299.

8. P. Frohman, "Vexing Problems in Forensic Medicine," *New York University Law Review*, Vol. XXXI (November, 1956), p. 1221.

9. Yale Kamisar, "Some Non-Religious Views Against Proposed 'Mercy Killing' Legislation," *Minnesota Law Review*, Vol. XXII (May, 1958), p. 1031.

10. Silving, "Euthanasia," *loc. cit.*, p. 354.

Chapter 3. CONFLICTING RELIGIOUS VIEWS

1. Karl Barth, *Church Dogmatics* (Edinburgh: T. & T. Clark, 1961), Vol. III/4, p. 126.

2. Dietrich Bonhoeffer, *Ethics* (The Macmillan Company, 1965), p. 145.

3. Joseph Fletcher, *Situation Ethics* (The Westminster Press, 1966), p. 33.

4. Paul Ramsey, *The Patient as Person* (Yale University Press, 1970), pp. 153, 157, 163. ———

5. *Ibid.*, pp. 159–160.

6. Joseph Fletcher, *Moral Responsibility* (The Westminster Press, 1967), p. 149.

7. *Ibid.*, p. 150.

8. Gerald A. Kelly, *Medico-Moral Problems* (St. Louis, Catholic Hospital Association of the U.S. & Canada, 1958), p. 128.

9. *Ibid.*, p. 129.

10. *Ibid.*

11. *Ibid.*

12. Edwin F. Healy, *Medical Ethics* (Loyola University Press, 1960), pp. 61–77; Charles J. McFadden, *Medical Ethics* (Philadelphia: F. A. Davis Company, 1961), pp. 227–247; Thomas J. O'Donnell, *Morals in Medicine* (The Newman Press, 1956), pp. 57, 66–68.

13. Joseph V. Sullivan, *The Morality of Mercy Killing* (The Newman Press, 1950), p. 72.

14. Bernard Häring, *Medical Ethics,* ed. by Gabrielle L. Jean (Fides Publishers, 1973), p. 147.

15. Ramsey, *The Patient as Person,* p. 151.

16. *Ibid.*, p. 132.

17. Barth, *Church Dogmatics,* Vol. III/4, p. 427.

18. Fletcher, *Moral Responsibility,* p. 154.

19. *Ibid.*, p. 155.

20. Bernard Bard and Joseph Fletcher, "The Right to Die," *The Atlantic Monthly,* Vol. CCXXI (April, 1968), p. 62.

21. Joseph Fletcher, "Ethics and Euthanasia," *American Journal of Nursing,* Vol. LXXIII (April, 1973), p. 670.

22. Healy, *Medical Ethics,* p. 396.

23. Kelly, *Medico-Moral Problems,* p. 118.

24. Sullivan, *The Morality of Mercy Killing,* p. 57.

25. *Ibid.,* p. 73.

26. Kelly, *Medico-Moral Problems,* p. 118; cf. Healy, *Medical Ethics,* p. 268.

27. Häring, *Medical Ethics,* pp. 146–150.

28. Daniel C. Maguire, "A Catholic View of Mercy Killing," *The Humanist,* Vol. XXXIV (July/August, 1974), p. 18.

29. Daniel C. Maguire, "Death, Legal and Illegal," *The Atlantic,* Vol. CXXXIII (February, 1974), p. 85.

30. Daniel C. Maguire, "Death by Chance, Death by Choice," *The Atlantic,* Vol. CXXXIII (January, 1974), p. 60.

31. Charles E. Curran, *Politics, Medicine, and Christian Ethics: A Dialogue with Paul Ramsey* (Fortress Press, 1973), pp. 161–162.

32. Ramsey, *The Patient as Person,* p. 153.

33. *Ibid.,* p. 162, n. 1.

34. *Ibid.,* p. 161.

35. Paul Ramsey, "The Indignity of 'Death with Dignity,' " *Hastings Center Studies,* Vol. II (May, 1974), p. 47.

36. Barth, *Church Dogmatics,* Vol. III/4, p. 398.

37. Paul Ramsey, *Deeds and Rules in Christian Ethics,* enlarged ed. (Charles Scribner's Sons, 1967), p. 71.

38. Barth, *Church Dogmatics,* Vol. III/4, p. 398.

39. Bonhoeffer, *Ethics,* p. 160.

40. Joseph Fletcher, *Morals and Medicine,* p. 176.

41. Bard and Fletcher, "The Right to Die," *loc. cit.,* p. 64.

42. H. Richard Niebuhr, *The Responsible Self* (Harper & Row, Publishers, Inc., 1963), pp. 48–56.

43. *Ibid.,* p. 60.

44. *Ibid.,* p. 144.

Chapter 4. MEDICAL DILEMMAS
IN TERMINAL CARE

1. W. Lloyd Warner, "The City of the Dead," *Death and Identity,* ed. by Robert L. Fulton (John Wiley & Sons, Inc., 1965), p. 374.

2. U.S. Bureau of Census, *Statistical Abstract of the United States: 1972* (Washington, D.C., 1973), p. 31.

3. Emil Bend and Thomas E. Callahan, "Artificial Heart Raises Real Hospital Issues," *Modern Hospital*, Vol. CVII (July, 1966), pp. 9–10.

4. J. M. Hinton, "The Physical and Mental Distress of Dying," *Quarterly Journal of Medicine*, Vol. XXXII (January, 1963), pp. 9–10.

5. Bend and Callahan, "Artificial Heart . . . ," *loc. cit.*, p. 593.

6. *Ibid.*, pp. 594–595.

7. *Ibid.*, p. 606.

8. Guy Owens, "Pain Management in Cancer," *New York Journal of Medicine*, Vol. LXVI (April 15, 1966), p. 958.

9. *Ibid.*; Bend and Callahan, "Artificial Heart . . . ," *loc. cit.*, p. 595.

10. Owens, "Pain Management in Cancer," *loc. cit.*, p. 959.

11. William P. Williamson, "Life or Death—Whose Decision?" *Journal of the American Medical Association*, Vol. CXCVII (Sept. 5, 1966), p. 149.

12. Hannibal Hamlin, "Life or Death by EEG," *Journal of the American Medical Association*, Vol. CXC (Oct. 12, 1964), pp. 120–121.

13. Charles W. Wahl, "The Fear of Death," in Herman L. Feifel, *The Meaning of Death* (McGraw-Hill Book Co., Inc., 1965), pp. 25–26.

14. Avery D. Weisman and Thomas P. Hackett, "Predilection to Death," in Robert L. Fulton (ed.), *Death and Identity* (John Wiley & Sons, Inc., 1965), p. 325.

15. Arnold A. Hutschnecker, "Personality Factors in Dying Patients," *The Meaning of Death* (McGraw-Hill Book Co., Inc., 1965), p. 237.

16. Wendell M. Swenson, "Attitudes Toward Death Among the Aged," in Robert L. Fulton (ed.), *Death and Identity* (John Wiley & Sons, Inc., 1965), pp. 110–111.

17. Daniel Cappon, "The Psychology of Dying" *Pastoral Psychology*, Vol. XII (February, 1961), pp. 36–37.

18. Erich Lindemann, "Symptomatology and Management of Acute Grief," in Robert L. Fulton (ed.), *Death and Identity* (John Wiley & Sons, Inc., 1965), pp. 188–189.

19. *Ibid.*, p. 195.

20. Weisman and Hackett, "Predilection to Death," *loc. cit.*, p. 321.

21. *Ibid.*, pp. 321–322.

22. Thomas S. Szasz, and Marc H. Hollender, "A Contribution to the Philosophy of Medicine," *Archives of Internal Medicine,* Vol. XCVII (1956), pp. 586–588.

23. Talcott Parsons, *Social Structure and Personality* (The Free Press of Glencoe, Inc., 1964), p. 340.

24. Szasz and Hollender, "A Contribution to the Philosophy of Medicine," *loc. cit.*, p. 586.

25. J. Russell Elkinton, "Medicine and the Quality of Life," *Annals of Internal Medicine,* Vol. LXIV (March, 1966), p. 13.

26. Charles S. Cameron, *The Truth About Cancer* (Prentice-Hall, Inc., 1956), pp. 115–116.

27. David A. Karnofsky, "Why Prolong the Life of a Patient with Advanced Cancer?" *Cancer Journal for Clinicians,* Vol. X (January–February, 1960), p. 9.

28. "Euthanasia Is Justified When . . . ?" *New Medical Materia* (October, 1962), pp. 31–32.

29. Norman K. Brown, Roger J. Bulger, E. Harold Laws, and Donovan I. Thompson, "The Preservation of Life," *Journal of the American Medical Association,* Vol. CCXI (Jan. 5, 1970), pp. 77–79.

30. Robert H. Williams, "Our Role in the Generation, Modification, and Termination of Life," *Journal of the American Medical Association,* Vol. CCIX (Aug. 11, 1969), pp. 914–917.

31. Sidney Shindell, "Legal and Ethical Problems in the Provision of Medical Care, II," *The Yale Journal of Biology and Medicine,* Vol. XXXVII (April, 1965), p. 404.

32. Charles K. Hofling, "Terminal Decisions," *Medical Opinion and Review* (October, 1966), p. 41.

33. "Seven Life-or-Death Dilemmas" (a symposium), *Medical Economics,* Vol. XLII (July 12, 1965), p. 102.

Chapter 5. THE LETTER OF THE LAW
AND THE SPIRIT OF MERCY

1. Philip E. Davis, *Moral Duty and Legal Responsibility* (Appleton-Century-Crofts, 1966), pp. 4–5.

2. *Ibid.*, p. 144.

3. *Ibid.*, pp. 43–44.

4. "Homicide," *Corpus Juris Secundum*, ed. by Donald J. Kiser (American Law Book Co., 1944), Vol. XL, secs. 97–98, pp. 956–957.

5. *Ibid.*, sec. 13, pp. 857–858.

6. The American Law Institute, *Model Penal Code*, Proposed Official Draft (Philadelphia: The American Law Institute, May 4, 1962), Art. 210–2, p. 125.

7. "Homicide," *loc. cit.*, sec. 40, pp. 898–899.

8. *Ibid.*, sec. 55, pp. 918–919.

9. *Ibid.*, sec. 62, pp. 924–929.

10. Burke Shartel and Marcus L. Plant (eds.), *The Law of Medical Practice* (Charles C Thomas, Publisher, 1959), pp. 371–372; cf. "Homicide," *loc. cit.*, secs. 20, 62–63, pp. 866–867, 928–929.

11. Shartel and Plant, *The Law of Medical Practice*, p. 119.

12. *Ibid.*, p. 115.

13. *Ibid.*, pp. 116–118.

14. *Ibid.*, pp. 4, 398–399.

15. American Medical Association, *Principles of Medical Ethics* (Chicago: American Medical Association, 1954), p. 15; cf. "Physicians and Surgeons," *Corpus Juris Secundum*, Vol. LXX, sec. 48, p. 959.

16. Shartel and Plant, *The Law of Medical Practice*, pp. 4–5; Anna Shinkle, "Consent to Medical and Surgical Treatment," *Drake Law Review*, Vol. XIV (May, 1965), p. 102.

17. Shartel and Plant, *The Law of Medical Practice*, pp. 399–400.

18. *Schloendorff* v. *Society of New York Hospital*, 211 N.Y., 125, 129, 105 N.E., 92, 93 (1914).

19. *Brooks Estate* v. *Brooks*, 33 U.S.L. Week 2486 (Ill. 1965);

Application of the President and Directors of Georgetown College, 331 F. 2d 1000 (D.C. Cir. 1964); cert. denied, 84 Sup. Ct. 1883 (1964); *Woods* v. *Brumlop,* 71 N.M. 221. 377 P. 2d 520, 524 (1962); *Natanson* v. *Kline,* 186 Kan. 393, 406–7, 350 P. 2d 1093, 1104 (1960).

20. Dan B. Dobbs, "Law and the Sick Room," *Saturday Review* (Aug. 3, 1968), pp. 43–44.

21. Shinkle, "Consent to Medical and Surgical Treatment," *loc. cit.,* pp. 107–108.

22. *Mohr* v. *Williams,* 95 Minn. 261, 104 N.W. 12 (1905).

23. *Pratt* v. *Davis,* 224 Ill. 300, 79 N.E. 562 (1906).

24. *Schloendorff* v. *Society of New York Hospital,* 211 N.Y. 125, 129, 125 N.E. 92, 93 (1914).

25. John Norman, "Physicians and Surgeons: Informed Consent," *Oklahoma Law Review,* Vol. XX (May, 1967), p. 215; Shinkle, "Consent to Medical and Surgical Treatment," *loc. cit.,* pp. 106–107.

26. Norman, "Physicians and Surgeons . . . ," *loc. cit.,* pp. 215–216.

27. *Salgo* v. *Leland Stanford Jr. University Board of Trustees,* 154 Cal. App. 2d 560, 578, 317, p. 2d 170, 181 (App. Dept. 1957).

28. *Salgo* v. *Leland Stanford Jr. University Board of Trustees,* 151 Cal. App. 2d 560, 578, 317, p. 2d 170, 181 (App. Dept. 1957).

29. *Watson* v. *Clutts,* 262 N.C. 153, 136 S.E. 2d 617, 621 (1964).

30. *Fischer* v. *Wilmington General Hospital,* 51 Del. 554, 149 A. 2d 749 (1959); *Ditlow* v. *Kaplan,* 181 So. 2d 226 (Fla. App. 1966); *Roberts* v. *Young,* 369 Mich. 133, 119 N.W. 2d 627 (1963).

31. *Mohr* v. *Williams,* 95 Minn. 261, 104 N.W. 12 (1905).

32. *Pratt* v. *Davis,* 224 Ill. 300, 79 N.E. 562 (1906).

33. *Jackovach* v. *Yocum,* 212 Iowa 914, 237, N.W. 444, 76 A.L.R. 551 (1931).

34. American Law Institute, *Restatement of The Law of Torts* (St. Paul: American Law Institute, 1965), sec. 62, pp. 94–95.

35. "Homicide," *loc. cit.,* sec. 13, pp. 857–858; sec. 37, pp. 896–898.

36. *State* v. *Beard,* 16 N.S. 50, 106 A-2d (1954); *State* v. *King,*

226 N.C. 214, 37 S.E. 2d 684 (1946); *State* v. *Ehlers.*, 98 N.J.L. 236; 119 A. 15 (1922).

37. *People* v. *Enwright*, 134 Cal. 527 at 530 66 p. 276 (1901).

38. *State* v. *Hombree*, 54 Ore. 463 at 474, 103 p. 1008 (1909); *Hedger* v. *State*, 144 W.S. 279, 128 N.W. 80 (1911).

39. William L. Burdick, *The Law of Crime* (Matthew Bender & Company, Inc., 1946), Vol. II, sec. 442, 447; Justin Miller, *Handbook of Criminal Law* (West Publishing Company, 1934), 55, 172; Rollin M. Perkins, *Criminal Law* (Foundation Press, Inc., 1957), p. 721; R. A. Anderson (ed.), *Wharton's Criminal Law and Procedure* (Rochester, N.Y.: Lawyer's Co-operative Publishing Company, 1957), Vol. I, sec. 194, 442.

40. "Homicide," *loc. cit.*, sec. 14, pp. 859–860.

41. *Turner* v. *State*, 119 Tenn. 663, 108 S.W. 1139 (1007).

42. *State* v. *Roberts*, 211 Mich. 185, 178, N.W. 690 (1920).

43. "Homicide," *loc. cit.*, secs. 62–63, pp. 928–929.

44. Shartel and Plant, *The Law of Medical Practice*, p. 372; "Homicide," *loc. cit.*, sec. 20, pp. 866–867.

45. George P. Fletcher, "Prolonging Life," *Washington Law Review*, Vol. XLII (June 1967), p. 1008.

46. "Homicide," *loc. cit.*, sec. 11, p. 856.

47. George P. Fletcher, "Prolonging Life," *loc. cit.*, p. 1008.

48. Excerpts from the transcript of the case, Glanville Williams, "Euthanasia and Abortion," *University of Colorado Law Review*, Vol. XXXVIII (Winter, 1966), p. 186 n.

49. *Repouille* v. *United States*, 165 F 2d 152, 153 (2d Cir. 1957).

50. Kamisar, "Some Non-Religious Views Against Proposed 'Mercy Killing' Legislation," *loc. cit.*, p. 972 n.

51. Harry Kalvin, Jr., "A Special Corner of Civil Liberties," *New York University Law Review*, Vol. XXXI (November, 1957), pp. 1236–1237.

52. Kamisar, *loc. cit.*, p. 974.

53. *Ibid.*, p. 1042.

54. Silving, "Euthanasia," *loc. cit.*, p. 354.

55. Norman St. John-Stevas, *Life, Death, and the Law: Law and Christian Morals in England and the United States* (Indiana University Press, 1961), pp. 336–339.

56. *Ibid.*, p. 338.

57. *Ibid.*, pp. 336–339.

58. *Ibid.*, p. 339.

59. *Ibid.*, p. 345.

60. Kamisar, *loc. cit.*, p. 976.

61. Silving, "Euthanasia," *loc. cit.*, pp. 360–363.

62. *Ibid.*, p. 387.

63. *Ibid.*, pp. 354–355.

64. *Ibid.*, pp. 358–359, 388–389.

65. *Ibid.*, pp. 388–389.

66. *Ibid.*, p. 388.

Chapter 6. NEW REQUIREMENTS OF CARE
FOR THE DYING

1. H. Richard Niebuhr, *Radical Monotheism and Western Culture* (Harper & Brothers, 1960), p. 112.

2. *Ibid.*, p. 32.

3. Ramsey, *Deeds and Rules*, p. 163.

4. Niebuhr, *The Responsible Self*, p. 142.

5. Hamlin, "Life or Death by EEG," *loc. cit.*, p. 113.

6. "Summit for the Heart," *Time*, Vol. XCII (July 26, 1968), p. 49.

7. Henry K. Beecher, "A Definition of Irreversible Coma," *Journal of the American Medical Association*, Vol. CCV (Aug. 5, 1968), pp. 85–88.

8. *Ibid.*

9. Ramsey, *The Patient as Person*, p. 161.

10. Thomas McKeown, "The Community's Responsibilities to the Malformed Child," Symposium on the Cost of Life, *Proceedings of the Royal Society of Medicine*, Vol. LX (November, 1967), p. 1220.

11. *Ibid.*

12. R. S. Illingworth and Cynthia M. Illingworth, "Thou Shalt Not Kill, Should Thou Strive to Keep Alive?" *Clinical Pediatrics*, Vol. IV (May, 1965), p. 307.

13. *Ibid.*, p. 308.

14. Denis Hill, "Economic and Ethical Considerations Arising from the Care of the Defective Child and the Very Old," Symposium on the Cost of Life, *Proceedings of the Royal Society of Medicine*, Vol. LX (November, 1967), p. 1233.

15. "Seven Authorities Discuss the Thalidomide Tragedy," *Illinois Medical Journal*, Vol. CXXII (September, 1962), p. 265.

16. McKeown, "The Community's Responsibilities to the Malformed Child," *loc. cit.*, pp. 1222–1223.

17. *Ibid.*, p. 1221.

18. *Ibid.*, p. 1222.

19. Illingworth and Illingworth, "Thou Shalt Not Kill . . . ," *loc. cit.*, p. 306.

20. *Ibid.*

21. Walter C. Alvarez, "Care of the Dying," *Journal of the American Medical Association*, Vol. CL (Sept. 13, 1952), p. 88.

22. *Ibid.*

23. *Ibid.*, p. 91.

24. Daniel Callahan, "The Sanctity of Life," in Donald R. Cutler (ed.), *The Religious Situation: 1969* (Beacon Press, 1969), pp. 300–301.

25. *Ibid.*, p. 314.

26. Marshall Houts and Irwin H. Houts (eds.), *Court Room Medicine*, Vol. III (Matthew Bender & Company, Inc., 1967), p. 1:14.

27. M. Martin Halley and William F. Harvey, "Medical vs. Legal Definitions of Death," *Journal of the American Medical Association*, Vol. CCIV (May 6, 1968), p. 424.

28. Hamlin, "Life or Death by EEG," *loc. cit.*, pp. 112–113.